ENGINEERING DEPARTMENT
TAUNTON TECHNICAL COLLEGE
WELLINGTON ROAD, TAUNTON

BOOK PRICE	s	d	BOOK NUMBER.	2

COURSE	STUDENT'S NAME	Date Issued

AN
INTRODUCTION TO THE
CLASSIFICATION OF ANIMALS

AN
INTRODUCTION TO THE
CLASSIFICATION OF ANIMALS

C. J. LERWILL BSc, MSc

CONSTABLE
LONDON

First published in 1971 by
Constable & Company Ltd
10 Orange Street London W C 2

Copyright © 1971 C. J. Lerwill

ISBN 0 09 457470 7 (*cloth*)
ISBN 0 09 457700 5 (*paper*)

Printed in Great Britain by
The Anchor Press Ltd., and bound by
Wm. Brendon & Son Ltd, both of Tiptree, Essex

CONTENTS

INTRODUCTION

Many General Certificate of Education Advanced Level courses in biological subjects now include a section on the variety of animal life, requiring breadth of study rather than depth. One of the purposes of this book is to provide such a survey of the animal kingdom. This forms the second part of this volume. The first part is devoted to a brief summary of the principles underlying the classification of animals, a topic often poorly understood by students, but so essential in the comparative study of life. A short appendix gives some basic information on the structure and use of identification keys.

At the end of this volume the reader will find a short list of works which contain, in greater detail, the principles of classification and surveys of the animal kingdom. The reader is referred especially to the book by Mayr, Linsley, and Usinger which covers the technicalities involved in taxonomic procedures in considerable depth.

I would like to express my gratitude to my colleagues for their comments on various aspects, and especially to my wife for her helpful criticisms throughout the preparation of the text.

PART I

THE PRINCIPLES OF CLASSIFICATION

I

HISTORICAL SKETCH

Descriptive zoology had its beginnings as long ago as the time of prehistoric man. The truth of this statement is borne out by the abundance of paintings in the caves inhabited by prehistoric man in various areas, particularly in the Mediterranean region. Prehistoric man's interest in animals and plants, however, was limited almost entirely to those organisms having a direct bearing on his livelihood. Apart from the vertebrate animals that were used for food or were dangerous to him, he also had some understanding of many invertebrates such as barnacles, mussels, seapens, winkles, cockles, oysters, clams, snails, and whelks. These organisms supplied him with spoons, knives, scrapers, jewellery, and 'money'. In order to survive, man had to be able to distinguish between, for example, those animals that were of use to him as food, and those that were a threat to his life. This, one could say, was the beginnings of the classification of animals. Various similar systems of practical taxonomy have been devised many times within historical time by natural philosophers the world over.

The earliest serious (academic) attempts to arrange living animals into groups were by the philosophers of the Mesopotamian civilization. Their studies were encouraged by the royal courts who were anxious to establish zoological gardens as prestige-boosting curiosities. Principal among these were the collections of the kings of Assur and Nineveh. Much of the classification, particularly of mammals, showed quite a high degree of accuracy. For instance, dogs, lions, jackals, cheetahs, badgers, and otters were grouped together in the 'dog family'; horses, mules, wild asses, dromedaries, and camels in the 'ass family'. However, there were many inaccuracies in their non-mammalian groups: orthopterous insects were grouped with the birds; eels were regarded, excusably, as snakes; and, rather surprisingly, tortoises were classified as fish.

The major contribution of the ancient world to the study of natural history was the work of the Greek philosopher Aristotle (384–322 B.C.). The writings of Aristotle were to influence the thoughts of natural historians right up to the eighteenth century. Unlike many of his contemporaries, Aristotle was only interested in those animals of which he had had personal experience. Thus he dismissed as mythical such animals as the elephant, camel, and hippopotamus. He proposed a system of classification dividing the animal world into the *Ennaima*, or blooded animals, and the *Anaima*, or bloodless animals. The *Ennaima* he divided into four groups—the viviparous quadrupeds, the oviparous quadrupeds, the birds, and the fishes. He recognized that cetaceans, seals, and bats were mammals, classifying them as viviparous quadrupeds. This group he further divided according to the structure of their skeletons and limbs. His oviparous quadrupeds consisted of the lizards, tortoises, and amphibians. The birds were divided into eight 'species' according to their food and the structure of their feet, and the fish were subdivided according to whether their skeleton was osseous or cartilaginous. Four groups were contained within the *Anaima*: soft-bodied invertebrates, soft-bodied invertebrates with hard shells, soft-bodied invertebrates with scales, and insects which were divided into nine groups.

4

There was little improvement on the Aristotelian classification until the seventeenth century; indeed, much of the work between the time of Aristotle and about A.D. 1600 was far inferior to that of Aristotle. During this period, however, many zoological collections were established throughout the world and numerous bestiaries appeared containing descriptions of many species (although a fair proportion of the species described were in fact mythical). The authors of these works rarely attempted to arrange their species in any systematic order apart from, in some cases, relating them to such human activities as agriculture and medicine. The Renaissance saw the exploration of many new lands and the discovery of many new species. The need for a standard classification of animals was becoming more and more essential, but because there was little agreement between authors, numerous independent systems of classification were developed.

The numerous systems devised were based on many and varied criteria. Paolo Giovio classified animals from a culinary point of view. Buffon based his classification on the degree of domestication, e.g. tame, ferine, sylvestrian. Some philosophers maintained that animals should be arranged in the order that God created them on the fifth and sixth days of creation. Others employed ecological criteria, dividing animals into swimmers, creepers, runners, fliers, or aquatic, subterranean, terrestrial, and aerial. Thus the group 'Aquatilia' included fish, various molluscs, marine worms, frogs, whales, sea-cows, beavers, etc.

During this period some attempts were made to return to Aristotle's anatomical and embryological criteria. 'Fish' were divided into soft fish, bony fish, and shell fish. Emiliano classified ruminants by the structure of their horns. Some divided tetrapods according to the structure and use of their limbs into quadrupeds, solipeds, digitates, talonates, waders, and palmipeds.

Between 1599 and 1616 Aldrovandi produced an encyclopedia in ten volumes containing a classification of the whole of the animal kingdom as he knew it. His scheme followed closely that of Aristotle, dividing the animal kingdom into two great groups, the blooded and bloodless. To Aristotle's four groups of blooded animals he added one group, 'Snakes and Dragons', which included not only such mythical creatures as sea-serpents, griffins, and harpies, but also malformed mammals such as two-headed sheep and men with webbed fingers. He classified the bloodless animals as follows:

1. Molluscs (cephalopods, sea-hares)
2. Testaceans (gastropods, bivalves, nautilis, barnacles, sea urchins)
3. Crustaceans (decapods only)
4. Insects: A. Terrestrial,
     i. Legged, a. Winged (winged insects)
               b. Wingless (wingless insects, and arachnids)
     ii. Legless (earthworms, tapeworms, slugs, roundworms)
          B. Aquatic,
     i. Legged (crustaceans other than decapods)
     ii. Legless (annelids, sea horses)
5. Zoophytes (corals, sea anemones, jelly-fish, sea cucumbers, sea squirts)

John Ray (1628–1705) also based his classification on that of Aristotle, but improved it by the use of many internal anatomical criteria such as the respiratory

6

organs of fish and the structure of the ventricle of amphibians.

The eighteenth century saw the publication of *Systema Naturae* by Linnaeus. This work contained descriptions of some 4370 species of animals, divided into six classes: Quadrupeds, Birds, Amphibians, Fishes, Insects, and Vermes. Linnaeus is remembered principally for the development of a standardized method of biological nomenclature, viz. the binomial system (see pages 16–17).

Until the eighteenth century most naturalists, including Linnaeus, believed in the fixity of species, i.e. that once a species had been formed it could not change. During the nineteenth century, principally due to the ideas of Charles Darwin and his *Origin of Species,* naturalists began to abandon the idea of the fixity of species and started to regard a species as a dynamic unit consisting of a population of individuals among which there is considerable variation, and which can change, even into new species, by natural selection of those variations which show the most advantageous adaptation to the changing environment. These ideas led to great specialization amongst zoologists. No longer were mammoth books produced attempting to describe as many species as possible. Zoologists took to studying single species, or groups of closely related species, learning as much about them as possible and attempting to determine their probable evolutionary relationships with other species.

Present-day taxonomy, *The New Systematics* of Julian Huxley, is the result of such investigations and takes into account the many facets of animal life, incorporating, for example, geographical, ecological, cytological, physiological, and genetical aspects. Whereas the old systematics was concerned with the type concept of a species which was regarded as immutable, the new systematics considers the population to be the important unit of a species consisting of many variable individuals. The type concept, however, is still of importance in the definition of species themselves.

2

FUNCTIONS AND PRINCIPLES
OF CLASSIFICATION

One of the main characteristics of man, distinguishing him from other animals, is his insatiable curiosity. His tremendous thirst for knowledge is not limited to a purely subjective view of his immediate surroundings. He is also interested in things which he has heard about but never actually seen and, perhaps more important, in ideas which have little or no bearing on his own life.

The accumulation of innumerable facts requires some system that makes order out of chaos. Thus we find, in every aspect of life, systems whereby facts are classified. The facts contained within this book are divided into chapters, each of which deals with one or more specific topics. A table of contents and an index are provided enabling the reader to find a particular fact quickly, without having to read the book from cover to cover each time. Offices have their filing cabinets; libraries arrange their volumes according to subject; roads are classified according to their use and quality.

It is natural for man, when confronted with more than a million species of animals, to classify them so as to form some system of reference. As mentioned earlier, primitive man classified animals according to their impact on his life, for example grouping species into harmless, dangerous, food suppliers, and so on. Later systems, however, were developed from a more objective viewpoint, grouping animals, not by their effect on man, but according to their structural similarities to one another. One of the consequences of such a classification system is the indication of the possible course of evolution and of the probable evolutionary relationships between species. The differences between similar species have arisen by evolutionary radiation from basic stock types. Thus the more alike two species are, the more closely related they are likely to be in evolutionary development. In a natural system of classification, the more alike two species are, the closer they are positioned in the orderly grouping of species. It follows, therefore, that a true system of classification tends to reflect the evolutionary relationships between species and groups.

A system of classification acts as a short-hand method of describing a species or a group. The example given below will suffice to indicate this function of classification.

KINGDOM Animalia
 SUBKINGDOM Metazoa
  PHYLUM Chordata
   SUBPHYLUM Vertebrata
    SUPERCLASS Gnathostomata
     CLASS Mammalia
      SUBCLASS Theria
       INFRACLASS Eutheria
        ORDER Rodentia
         SUBORDER Myomorpha
          FAMILY Cricetidae
           SUBFAMILY Cricetinae
            TRIBE Cricetini
             e.g. *Mesocricetus auratus,* the
             golden hamster.

Each of the groups into which an animal is placed gives us more and more information about the species in question. The classification of the golden hamster gives us the following information about the species. Only a few of the characteristics of each group are included; a complete classification and a full description of each category would be very extensive and would ultimately give a complete, precise description of the species concerned.

KINGDOM Animalia: possessing typical animal characteristics; holozoic nutrition.

SUBKINGDOM Metazoa: multicellular with the cells organized into tissues.

PHYLUM Chordata: possessing gill slits, notochord, and dorsal, hollow central nervous system, at least for part of life.

SUBPHYLUM Vertebrata: notochord wholly or partially replaced by cartilaginous or bony material forming vertebral column.

SUPERCLASS Gnathostomata: possessing articulating jaws of bony material.

CLASS Mammalia: possessing pentadactyl limbs, bony skeleton, hair, mammary glands, four-chambered heart; gill slits in embryo only.

SUBCLASS Theria: mammary glands with well-developed nipples; viviparous.

INFRACLASS Eutheria: young develop in uterus attached to mother by allantoic placenta.

ORDER Rodentia: gnawing mammals with one pair of long incisors in each jaw; incisors with enamel on front surface only; dentition incomplete—canines absent, and tendency to reduction in number of cheek teeth.

SUBORDER Myomorpha: tibia and fibula of hind limbs fused; zygomatic arches of skull slender.

FAMILY Cricetidae: dentition reduced to sixteen

teeth – no premolars; mainly ground-dwelling rodents of small size.

SUBFAMILY Cricetinae: molars of limited growth, with two rows of tubercules.

TRIBE Cricetini: thickset body with short legs and short tail; cheek pouches present.

e.g. *Mesocricetus auratus,* the golden hamster.

Classification is of importance in the comparative study of animals. A detailed study of one species can give information which applies not only to that particular species but also, with modifications, to other species. The usefulness of classification in this respect is that it indicates the extent of evolutionary divergence, and hence the probable magnitude of dissimilarity between species, and thus assists in the extrapolation of information from one species to another.

The identification and classification of a species involves an investigation of the characteristics of that species, comparison with other species, and finally the positioning of the species in the order of classification such that its evolutionary relationships to other species are indicated. In the investigation of the characteristics, ideally, all possible characteristics should be included – structural, physiological, ecological, behavioural, etc. It is convenient, however, to concentrate on some types of characteristic more than on others. Generally, structural characteristics are used for the basis of classification. It is more satisfactory to use structure where possible since structural features are present at all times. Identifications are often made using dead specimens.

Within any one group it is usual to use a particular trait for identification and classification. Thus the major classification of the vertebrates can be based principally on the structure of the skeleton. The classification of mammals depends to a large extent on the features of the skull, particularly of the teeth. In most cases it is safe to use only a few characteristics in defining a group as past experience has shown that animals with these particular characteristics will also possess other characteristics in common with the group. Thus, if one is presented with a mammal with a pair of unbranched, permanent horns, one is reasonably safe in assuming that it is a member of the family Bovidae of the order Artiodactyla, and therefore also has the following characteristics: fused ulna and fibula; fused foot bones forming 'cannon-bone'; ruminant animal with four-chambered stomach; dental formula – I o/3, C o/1, PM 3/3, M 3/3; etc.

The system of classification is such that primary characteristics tend to be used for grouping in the higher categories, and secondary characteristics for the lower categories. For example, the superficial features of whales which show resemblances to fish are secondary characteristics developed for life in a similar habitat. The primary characteristics of whales are those features which show that they are in fact mammals. The secondary characteristics are sufficient to warrant the establishment of the order Cetacea distinguishing the whales from other mammals. Similarly, the primary characteristics of bats are of a mammalian nature, although their secondary features (i.e. fore limbs adapted for flight) show some resemblance to bird habit.

The descriptions of species often refer to 'typical' specimens. A species, however, consists of a population of individuals in various stages of development. Within a population there can be considerable variation amongst its members. In many species there is a distinguishable difference between the sexes. Some species, e.g. cattle, may have intersexes (individuals with characteristics intermediate between the two sexes). Gynandromorphs (individuals with some male tissue and some female tissue) can occur, e.g. in some insects. Some organisms have more than one form during the life cycle, e.g. polyp and medusa forms in cnidarians. In some insects different types of adult are produced, e.g. queens, workers, and drones in bees. Other variations can occur in relation to season, climate, habitat, and so on. Occasionally these variants, when first discovered, are described as separate species, and it is only at a later date that their true relationships are determined. This is particularly so in the case of larval forms.

To summarize the present chapter, the functions of a natural classification of animals are: a) to arrange the million or so species into some meaningful system of reference, b) to act as a short-hand method of describing species and groups, and c) to assist in the identification of specimens. The outcome of such a system is that it indicates possible evolutionary relationships and aids the comparison of species.

3

UNITS OF CLASSIFICATION

Species and Genus

The basic taxonomic unit, or taxon, is the species. A species is what one normally thinks of as a 'kind' of animal or plant. In the majority of cases a species can be defined as a group of naturally, or potentially naturally, interbreeding animals or plants. Animals of a species are capable of breeding with others of the same species, but not normally with those of other species. A species is thus a reproductively isolated group of individuals. Difficulties may arise with the use of this definition, for instance in the case of ring species, an example of which is shown by the herring gull and lesser black-backed gull in Britain. These two forms are at the two ends of a single chain of subspecies encompassing the northern hemisphere. Each subspecies may interbreed with its neighbouring subspecies, but in the case of these gulls, the two ends of the chain occur in Britain, the two types co-exist and do not interbreed, and are therefore considered to be separate species. Further difficulties arise with those animals in which sexual reproduction does not occur, e.g. in some Protozoa, and with some apparent species which will produce hybrid forms although such offspring are usually infertile.

The members of a given species are similar to each other except for natural variation of detail. However, the various natural variations within a species may become differentially accentuated in localized regions, such that the members of a species in a particular area may be recognizably distinct from members of the same species within a different area. In these cases different subspecies may be named on the basis of these variations. The subspecies nevertheless still belong to the same species and are capable of breeding with each other. The short-tailed vole belongs to the species *Microtus agrestis*. A number of subspecies are recognized in Britain: the voles of this species in England and the Scottish Lowlands are of the subspecies *Microtus agrestis hirtus,* those in the Scottish Highlands are *Microtus agrestis neglectus,* those in the North-West Highlands of Scotland and in the Hebrides are *Microtus agrestis exsul.* All these subspecies are capable of interbreeding with one another, although in their natural environment they are unlikely to come into contact with one another. Indeed, this isolation was the factor which allowed natural selection to occur along slightly different lines in these areas. The formation of a subspecies is no doubt the initial stage in the development of new, separate, species. If separate subspecies continue to develop in isolation, their differences may, in time, become such that they are no longer capable of interbreeding. The subspecies would then be considered as separate species.

As may be seen from the name of the short-tailed vole given above, the name of a species of animal (the binomen) consists of two words. The first word, *Microtus* in the above example, is known as the generic name, indicating the genus to which the animal belongs, while the second, *agrestis* in the above example, is known as the specific name. A genus consists of a number (in some cases only one) of species which show a close resemblance to one another.

At this point a few of the conventions involved in the naming of animals may be mentioned. All species described must be named in accordance with the International Rules of Zoological Nomenclature drawn up by the International Commission of Zoological Nomenclature which receives its authority from successive International Congresses of Zoology.

The scientific name of a species must consist of two words (binomen), and that of a subspecies of three words (trinomen). The words used must be in Latin or in a Latinized form, and usually bear some relation to the characteristics of the animals. The generic name must be in the nominative singular and be written with a capital initial letter. The specific name should normally be written with a lower-case initial letter. Strictly, the name of an animal should be followed by the name, or the abbreviated name, of the author who first gave the animal that name. This should then be followed by the year of naming, e.g. *Canis lupus* Linnaeus, 1758. The accepted name of an animal should be the first name given to the animal since 1st January, 1758, the year of publication of the tenth edition of Linnaeus' work, *Systema Naturae*. On occasions it may be desirable to change the generic category of a species. It may be decided, for instance, that two species, previously of the same genus, show sufficient divergence to warrant their division into two separate genera. If the generic name of a species is changed, the name of the original describer should be placed in parentheses. Thus the golden hamster was originally named *Cricetus auratus* by Waterhouse, but it was later decided that this species should be placed in a different genus from the European hamster, *Cricetus cricetus*. The name of the golden hamster was thus changed from *Cricetus auratus* Waterhouse, to *Mesocricetus auratus* (Waterhouse). Convention has it that in print the scientific name of an animal (but not the name of the author) should be printed in italic lettering. When one is writing by hand one should underline the name, the convention for indicating italics.

In each species the original specimen (or group of specimens) used for the original description is designated as the type-specimen. The type-specimen acts as a point of reference for the indentification of individuals. There are various categories of type-specimens:

1. Primary types – these are the original specimens used in describing a new species. The basic primary type is the holotype – an original single specimen. In some cases the original description is based on a group of specimens which are termed syntypes, without any particular individual being selected as the holotype. One of the syntypes later selected as the type specimen is known as the lectotype. The remainder of the syntypes are then referred to as paratypes.

2. Supplementary types – these are specimens used to add to, or correct, descriptions of previously described species. The principal category of supplementary type is the neotype – a specimen selected to replace the primary type when this is no longer available.

3. Typical specimens, e.g. topotype, metatype. These are individuals of a species that have not been used in connection with the published descriptions of a species, and which may, therefore, show variations from such descriptions.

In each genus a particular species is designated as the type-species. The type-species acts as a point of reference for the genus. A genus is limited to those species which resemble the type-species of that genus more than the type-species of any other genus.

The Family

Just as a number of closely related species are grouped in a genus, closely related genera are grouped in families. A family is delimited by a type-genus. Thus, as in the case of the type-species of a genus, a family consists of those genera which resemble the type-genus of that family more than the type-genera of other families. Closely related families may be grouped together in a single super-family. A family may be divided into a number of sub-families which, in a few groups, particularly Crustacea and Mammalia, may be further divided into a number of tribes. The name of a family consists of the stem of the name of the type-genus with the ending *-idae*; that of a subfamily consists of the stem of the name of the type-genus of the subfamily, which may or may not be the same as the type-genus of the family, with the ending *-inae*. Similarly, the name of a tribe ends in *-ini,* and that of a superfamily in *-oidea*. The system is illustrated in the following example which shows the systematic position of two of the tribes of the squirrel family.

SUPERFAMILY Sciuroidea
FAMILY Sciuridae
SUBFAMILY Sciurinae
TRIBE Sciurini
    Type-genus: *Sciurus*
TRIBE Tamiasciurini
    Type-genus: *Tamiasciurus*

In this example the genus *Sciurus* is the type-genus of the tribe, subfamily, family, and superfamily. Thus the stem of the word, *Sciur-,* is used for the names of these categories, with the appropriate suffixes. The genus

Tamiasciurus is the type-genus only of the tribe to which it belongs, i.e. the tribe Tamiasciurini.

The ruling of the International Commission is that these endings should not be used for categories other than those specified. However, the ending *-oidea* has been in use for some time for a few groups at levels other than the superfamily. Many zoologists are reluctant to amend this, and thus the ending *-oidea* is still in use for groups such as the echinoderms in which the classes are still normally referred to as Crinoidea, Asteroidea, Ophiuroidea, Echinoidea, and Holothuroidea. Other groups described in this book for which this ending is commonly used are the phylum Echiuroidea, the class Planctosphaeroidea of the hemichordates, and the order Hyracoidea of the mammals.

The Higher Categories

The taxa below the superfamily level are defined by type-genera and type-species as described above. The function of these categories is to indicate similarities between distinct species. The categories above the superfamily level are not delimited by types, and are based less on similarities and more on the differences in basic form. Above the superfamily, the major levels of classification, in ascending order, are: order, class, and phylum. As with the lower levels, these taxa may be prefixed by sub- and super-, thereby considerably increasing the possible number of levels of classification. Phyla are the major divisions of the animal kingdom. All the animals within a phylum, although showing a very wide range of form, should possess a common basic body plan. There are no rules laid down for the naming of the categories above the level of the superfamily.

The standard taxonomic categories are shown in the list.

KINGDOM
  Subkingdom
  PHYLUM
    Subphylum
    Superclass
      CLASS
       Subclass
        Superorder
        ORDER
         Suborder
         Superfamily
         FAMILY
          Subfamily
           Supergenus
           GENUS
            Subgenus
            SPECIES
             Subspecies

Not all of these need be used in the classification of any particular group. The essential categories are shown in bold type. A few other categories are sometimes used in particular groups. It has been mentioned previously that the category Tribe may be used in the classification of Crustacea and Mammalia. In the classification of the Insecta the term Division may be used between Subclass and Order. The accepted classification of mammals includes the terms Infraclass after Subclass, and Cohort between Infraclass and Order.

4

RECENT TECHNIQUES IN TAXONOMY

The classification of animals, at present, is based mainly on structural features, external and internal, which are visible to the naked eye, and there tends to be *a priori* weighting of characteristics – particular characters are selected as being of greatest importance and use in the classification of a particular group. In the present chapter, three recent developments in taxonomy are briefly surveyed. The first, numerical taxonomy, attempts to overcome the 'weighting' problem by considering a large number of characteristics, none of them being given preferential treatment. The other two techniques consider only single characteristics, and are thus extreme cases of *a priori* weighting. Serotaxonomy is concerned with the comparison of the proteins of the body fluids of animals. Such proteins are very stable within a species, and they are direct products of the genetic material, generally not modified by developmental and environmental influences, as are many of the grosser structural features. Although these studies give an indication of differences in genetic material, only a few genes are involved in the production of the proteins concerned. Genetic comparisons are taken further in DNA-hybridization studies, involving the direct comparison of the genetic material from different species.

Of these three techniques, numerical taxonomy offers a completely new method for the classification of animals, while serotaxonomy is of particular use where other methods of classification do not give clear indications of relationships. DNA-hybridization should, theoretically, offer the ultimate in taxonomic methods. However, due to the difficulties involved, this seems unlikely in the near future.

Numerical Taxonomy

As mentioned in Chapter 2, in the classification of species, ideally as many characteristics as possible should be used. However, the more features used, the more complex becomes the comparison between species; thus the number of features used is limited by the time required to analyse the data and by the comprehension of the complexity one is creating. For this reason there has been a tendency to use only a few characters in the descriptions of species. This then presents the problem of selecting those characteristics which are of greatest importance and use. With the advent of electronic computers, however, the use of a large number of characteristics was made possible. Thus the branch of taxonomy known as 'numerical taxonomy' has been developed.

Numerical taxonomy is only involved with resemblance between species; as far as possible, no differential treatment is given to any one trait. In simple terms the system is as follows. The specimens to be compared are referred to as 'operational taxonomic units' (OTUs), and the features as 'unit characters'. It is desirable to have as many unit characters as possible, preferably at least forty. The data are constructed such that unit characters are recorded either in a graded system, i.e. 0, 1, 2, 3, etc. (for instance, the tails of rodents could be graded: absent 0, very short 1, medium length 2, very long 3), or simply as absence (0) or presence (1) (for example, absence or presence of an enzyme). The data are then programmed so that all possible pairs of OTUs are compared by the computer with respect to each unit character.

From the data, similarity coefficients between all possible pairs of OTUs are obtained. The similarity coefficient can be calculated from the formula:*

$$S = \frac{100a}{a+b+c}\%,$$ where 'a' is the number of

unit characters common to the two OTUs in question, 'b' is the number possessed by one only, and 'c' is the number possessed by the other alone. Thus a similarity

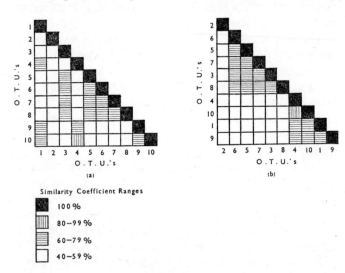

FIGURE I

Similarity matrices of hypothetical similarity coefficient ranges for a group of ten OTUs, a) showing the data before re-ordering of the OTUs, and b) after cluster analysis showing grouping of the OTUs.

* The formula, in this simple form, can only be applied where the data are in the form 0 or 1.

coefficient of 100% shows total similarity, while one of 0% indicates total dissimilarity. Cluster analysis can then be applied to the results. Arbitary ranges of similarity co-efficients are chosen to represent taxonomic units, which are called 'phenons' to avoid confusion with the conventional taxa. The similarity coefficient results are represented in the form of a similarity matrix (see Figure 1 (a)). These are then rearranged to form clusters (see Figure 1 (b)), which can then be interpreted in the form of a phenogram (see Figure 2).

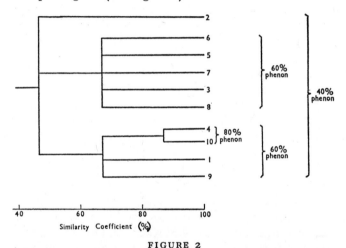

FIGURE 2

Phenogram based on the information shown in Figure 1 showing the hierarchical grouping of the ten OTUs and the phenetic levels.

Numerical methods of taxonomy are of most use at the present time in connection with molecular and biochemical systematics where large numbers of unit characters are obtained, and are being widely used in taxonomic studies of bacteria.

Serotaxonomy

Whereas numerical taxonomy considers a large number of characteristics, serotaxonomy is concerned with only one feature, the similarities of the proteins in the body fluids. The results of serological investigations correspond with conventional methods of taxonomy in cases where relationships are already well established, and it can thus be assumed that serological reactions give reasonable indications of relationships, especially within the lower levels of classification. The techniques are of particular use where relationships are not well established by other means.

Serum, or other body fluids containing antigenic proteins, from one species is injected into a suitable host, usually the rabbit, in which antibodies develop, specific to the introduced antigens. Serum (containing specific antibodies) from the host, if then mixed with antigenic protein from the original donor species, will give a maximum precipitate (homologous precipitin reaction). This is regarded as a standard, with which the reaction with antigens from another species (heterologous precipitin reaction) can be compared. Close evolutionary relationship between the donor species and the test species is indicated by similar precipitin reactions. Distant relationships are indicated by less precipitate in the heterologous reaction.

The degree of precipitation can be estimated by a number of methods. Values are often measured and quoted in the form of the greatest dilution which produces the heterologous precipitate as a percentage of that for the homologous reaction. Other methods involve the measurement of the precipitate itself by, for example, turbidometry, or measurement of unprecipitated protein by the determination of nitrogen concentration. More recently techniques of gel diffusion and immunoelectrophoresis have been used. These methods involve the diffusion of the antigens and the antibodies towards one another through an agar gel, characteristic patterns of precipitation being formed where the two meet (see Figure 3).

At the phylum level, such investigations have indi-

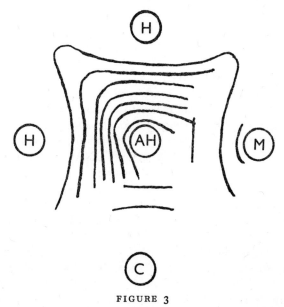

FIGURE 3

Diagram of the precipitin lines formed in an immunodiffusion test on an agar-gel plate. The centre well (AH) contained anti-human serum. The outer wells contained sera from: human (H); clawed bird, *Meriones unguiculatus*, (M); and striped hamster, *Cricetulus barabensis*, (C). The precipitin lines to the top and left show the homologous reaction, those to the right and bottom show the heterologous reaction.

cated, for instance, that the hemichordates are more akin to the echinoderms than to the annelids, and that the molluscs have a closer relationship with the annelids than with the arthropods. Serological studies have been used mainly to investigate lower levels of classification, particularly those of mammals. Lagomorphs show greater serological correspondence with artiodactyls than with rodents, although many of their morphological characteristics show similarities with the latter. At the species level, studies on the giant panda, the systematic position of which is uncertain, show greater similarity with bears than with raccoons.

DNA-Hybridization

Since the basic characteristics of an organism are determined by the genetic make-up of the nucleic acids, and since evolutionary change is brought about by changes in the genetic constitution of individuals, direct comparison of the deoxyribonucleic acids (DNA) of individuals should give accurate indications of evolutionary relationships. During the last ten years, techniques of DNA-hybridization have been developed, which allow direct comparison of the DNA from different species.

Isolated, double-stranded DNA, if heated to 100°C, will separate into single strands. On slowly cooling, the strands will recombine, once again giving the double-stranded form. DNA-hybridization involves the mixing of different samples of single-stranded DNA. If the two samples are of sufficient similarity, hybrid double strands will be formed, and the degree of hybridization is then determined. This determination can be carried out by a number of methods. In studies on bacteria, one species is grown on nutrients containing the heavy nitrogen–15 isotope as the sole source of nitrogen, such that the DNA of this species will, after a number of generations, become 'heavy' DNA. Determination of hybridization can then be carried out by comparing the settling of the various fractions in density-gradients using an ultracentrifuge.

Techniques with higher organisms involve the use of radioactive isotopes, which are introduced into the DNA in place of the naturally occurring stable isotopes. The degree of hybridization can then be determined by separating the various fractions of the mixture, and measuring their radioactivity. DNA from one species is heated to separate the strands, cooled quickly, and suspended in an agar gel to prevent recombination. DNA from another species is rendered radioactive, for instance by tissue culture using carbon–14 or phosphorus–32 isotopes as sources of carbon or phosphorus, broken down into fragments, and then separated into single-stranded fragments. This is then added to the agar gel containing single-stranded DNA from the first species. Following incubation, the radioactive fractions are isolated and their radioactive counts recorded. From this information, the degree of hybridization can be determined.

As with numerical taxonomy and serotaxonomy, the data obtained from DNA-hybridization studies, on the whole, corresponds with conventional methods of taxonomy. For example, the mouse has a little less DNA similarity to the hamster than to the rat, and considerably less to the guinea pig. This corresponds with the conventional classification of these animals, in which the mouse and rat are placed in the same family (Muridae), and the hamster in the family Cricetidae. Both of these families are within the same suborder (Myomorpha). The guinea pig is placed in a separate suborder (Hystricomorpha), within the same order (Rodentia). Some results, however, do not quite agree with conventional methods. It would seem that the degree of difference between mouse DNA and guinea pig DNA is of the same order as that between mouse DNA and rabbit DNA. The rabbit is placed in the order Lagomorpha, and thus the structure of the order Rodentia would seem to be in doubt, as there would appear to be as much difference *within* it as there is *between* it and the order Lagomorpha.

The techniques of DNA-hybridization are, at present, in the early stages of development. Many refinements are necessary and, due to the complexities of the methods in the isolation of DNA samples and the radioactive labelling, it is unlikely that studies of DNA-hybridization will be widely used by taxonomists. Those studies which are made, however, will provide supplementary data of use in classification.

PART II

A SURVEY OF THE ANIMAL KINGDOM

INTRODUCTION

The various phyla into which the animal kingdom is divided represent differing grades of organization. The order in which the phyla are normally presented gives an overall picture of increasing complexity and evolutionary development. This is not to say that particular species of a 'lowly' phylum are necessarily less complex themselves than particular species of a 'higher' phylum, but that the grade of organization of a 'lowly' phylum is less complex and less advanced in evolutionary terms than that of a 'higher' phylum.

Each phylum is characterized by a different basic body plan (see Table 1) and a pattern of increasing evolutionary development can be traced through the phyla:

1. *Cell number*. All the phyla except the Protozoa consist of multicellular animals. The body is made up of a number of cells, each of which is an integral part of the individual. The protozoan body is not made up of a number of cells but consists of one such unit. The Protozoa can be regarded either as unicellular or as acellular depending on one's definition of a cell. There are two fundamentally distinct definitions of a cell. A cell can be defined as consisting of a nucleus and that portion of cytoplasm over which the nucleus has immediate control, in which case the Protozoa must be regarded as unicellular; or, a cell can be defined as a unit of protoplasm within an individual, in which case the Protozoa must be regarded as acellular since the protozoan body is not divided up into such units.

Phylum		Grade 1	Grade 2	Grade 3	Coelom	Protostomia / Deuterostomia	Coelom type
Protozoa	Unicellular	Protoplasmic					
Mesozoa	Multicellular	Cellular					
Porifera	Multicellular	Cellular					
Cnidaria	Multicellular	Tissue	Diploblastica Radiata				
Ctenophora	Multicellular	Tissue	Diploblastica Radiata				
Platyhelminthes	Multicellular	Organ-System	Triploblastica Bilateria	Acoelomata			
Nemertea	Multicellular	Organ-System	Triploblastica Bilateria	Acoelomata			
Acanthocephala	Multicellular	Organ-System	Triploblastica Bilateria	Pseudocoelomata			
Aschelminthes	Multicellular	Organ-System	Triploblastica Bilateria	Pseudocoelomata			
Entoprocta	Multicellular	Organ-System	Triploblastica Bilateria	Coelomata	Protostomia	Lophophorata
Phoronida	Multicellular	Organ-System	Triploblastica Bilateria	Coelomata	Protostomia	Lophophorata
Ectoprocta	Multicellular	Organ-System	Triploblastica Bilateria	Coelomata	Protostomia	Lophophorata
Brachiopoda	Multicellular	Organ-System	Triploblastica Bilateria	Coelomata	Protostomia	Lophophorata
Sipunculida	Multicellular	Organ-System	Triploblastica Bilateria	Coelomata	Protostomia	Schizocoelomata
Echiuroidea	Multicellular	Organ-System	Triploblastica Bilateria	Coelomata	Protostomia	Schizocoelomata
Mollusca	Multicellular	Organ-System	Triploblastica Bilateria	Coelomata	Protostomia	Schizocoelomata
Annelida	Multicellular	Organ-System	Triploblastica Bilateria	Coelomata	Protostomia	Schizocoelomata
Arthropoda	Multicellular	Organ-System	Triploblastica Bilateria	Coelomata	Protostomia	Schizocoelomata
Echinodermata	Multicellular	Organ-System	Triploblastica Bilateria	Coelomata	Deuterostomia	Enterocoelomata
Chaetognatha	Multicellular	Organ-System	Triploblastica Bilateria	Coelomata	Deuterostomia	Enterocoelomata
Pogonophora	Multicellular	Organ-System	Triploblastica Bilateria	Coelomata	Deuterostomia	Enterocoelomata
Hemichordata	Multicellular	Organ-System	Triploblastica Bilateria	Coelomata	Deuterostomia	Enterocoelomata
Chordata	Multicellular	Organ-System	Triploblastica Bilateria	Coelomata	Deuterostomia	Enterocoelomata

TABLE 1. BASIC STRUCTURAL GRADES WITHIN THE ANIMAL KINGDOM

2. *Subkingdoms.* The multicellular phyla are divided into one main group and two minor groups. These groups are given the rank of subkingdoms. The subkingdoms Mesozoa and Parazoa each contain but a single phylum, Mesozoa and Porifera respectively. These two groups are considered to be somewhat abortive side branches of evolution, being early divergences from the main line of evolutionary development, although the evolutionary position of the Mesozoa is at present uncertain. Some authorities regard the group as an abortive attempt at multicellularity by the Protozoa; others consider the mesozoans to be degenerate Platyhelminthes. The remainder of the multicellular phyla are all included in the subkingdom Metazoa. The animal kingdom is thus divided into four subkingdoms – Protozoa, Mesozoa, Parazoa, and Metazoa.

3. *Levels of differentiation and organization.* The Protozoa are at a protoplasmic level of organization in that differentiation within the organism is within the protoplasm itself. The Mesozoa and Parazoa are at a cellular level of organization. The cells constituting the individual are not all the same but are differentiated for the performance of different functions. There is, however, very little, if any, co-ordination between the cells. Some of the poriferans, however, approach a tissue level of organization, the level shown by the phyla Cnidaria and Ctenophora. In such organisms similar cells are aggregated into tissues, the activities of the cells of a tissue being co-ordinated to provide unification of function. All the other phyla are at an organ level of organization. Various tissues combine to form organs, each of which usually has one principal function. The organs themselves are united forming a number of systems, e.g. alimentary, nervous, reproductive systems.

4. *Germ layers and symmetry*. Of the Metazoa, the most primitive body plan is exhibited by the Cnidaria and Ctenophora. In these the body wall is made up of two cellular layers, the ectoderm and endoderm, separated by a somewhat structureless mesoglea. The symmetry of the body is of a radial nature, while in the rest of the Metazoa symmetry is basically bilateral, although there are some cases of secondary radial symmetry. In these, the majority of the Metazoa, the body wall consists of three cellular germ layers, ectoderm, mesoderm, and endoderm. It is within the mesoderm that most of the organ systems of the body are formed. Due to these differences in germ layers and symmetry, the Metazoa can be divided into two groups. The Cnidaria and Ctenophora comprise the Radiata or Diploblastica, and the rest of the Metazoa comprise the Bilateria or Triploblastica.

5. *The coelom*. The triploblastic phyla may be further divided with respect to the absence or presence of a coelom, and its form. In the Platyhelminthes and Nemertea the space between the ectoderm and endoderm is completely filled with mesodermal material and there is thus no coelom. These two phyla may therefore be grouped together as the Acoelomata. In all the other triploblastic phyla a cavity is present within the body between the ectoderm and endoderm. This can have one of two basic forms. In the Acanthocephala, Aschelminthes, and Entoprocta the cavity is lined by the ectoderm and endoderm, and the mesoderm is accumulated in specific regions. These three phyla may be referred to as the Pseudocoelomata. In the remaining phyla the mesoderm forms two basic layers: a layer of somatic mesoderm lines the inner side of the ectoderm, and a layer of splanchnic mesoderm lines the outer side of the endoderm, with the

result that the coelom is bounded by mesoderm and is not in direct contact with the ectoderm and endoderm. These phyla constitute the Coelomata. These may be further divided with respect to the formation of the coelom (see 7 below).

6. *Embryology*. The Coelomata may be divided into two groups by virtue of their embryonic development. Most of the invertebrate coelomate phyla can be grouped as the Protostomia. In these the mouth develops at the position of the embryonic blastopore. Cleavage of the egg is determinate and spiral or a modification of this pattern. The remainder of the invertebrate coelomate phyla and also the Chordata may be grouped as the Deuterostomia in which it is the anus that develops at the position of the blastopore, and cleavage is typically indeterminate and radial or bilateral.

7. *Coelom development*. The Coelomata may be divided into three groups on differences in the formation of the coelom and on the presence or absence of a lophophore. In the deuterostomial coelomates the mesoderm and coelom develop as hollow pouches from the gut. This is known as enterocoelous development. In five of the protostomial phyla the mesoderm rises as a solid mass between the ectoderm and endoderm, and this then splits to form the coelom. Such development is called schizocoelous. In the remaining three protostomial phyla, coelom development is by a variety of ways but is not enterocoelous or schizocoelous. Their larvae are not of the trochosphere type as is typical for the schizocoelous groups. The principal characteristic that these three phyla have in common is the possession of a lophophore, which consists of ciliated, coelomate tentacles surrounding

the mouth and used in food capture. Hence these three phyla are known as the lophophorate coelomates.

8. *Metameric segmentation*. True metameric segmentation occurs in only a few phyla, principally in the Annelida and Arthropoda of the protostomial coelomates and in the Chordata (except the urochordates) of the deuterostomial coelomates. The evolutionary development of segmentation occurred independently in protostomes and deuterostomes.

The aim of the survey of the animal kingdom that follows is to give an indication of the variety of form to be found within the animal kingdom, and to show how the multitude of species is divided up into taxonomic groups. The definitions given for each group indicate the basic characteristics of the animals within that group. In many cases individual species do not conform to all the characteristics given for the group, which should be regarded, in the main, as the characteristics of 'typical' individuals. The definitions given for each group are kept as brief as possible, and as far as possible give only those characteristics most readily discernible. The examples of genera given for each group include both 'typical' and 'atypical' types and indicate the range of form within the group. Only those groups containing species living today are included in the survey, and all the examples given are present-day forms.

THE ANIMAL KINGDOM

The plant and animal kingdoms can normally be distinguished by their methods of nutrition, and the lack of cellulose cell walls in the animal kingdom. Plants are able to manufacture their own food substances from inorganic material by means of photosynthesis. Such nutrition is termed holophytic or autotrophic. Animals on the other hand require a source of complex organic compounds. This type of nutrition is termed holozoic or heterotrophic. The distinction between the animal and plant kingdoms at the 'lowly' levels of life, however, is not precise. One group mentioned below can be considered as belonging to either kingdom. This group, the Phytomastigina, contains organisms which possess both animal and plant characteristics. Many are capable of photosynthesis, although some of these are able to live holozoically under certain conditions. However, since animals and plants probably had a common origin, one would expect to find organisms with characteristics of both types, which could be classified in either kingdom depending on the characteristics used for their classification. It must, of course, be remembered that classification is a system imposed upon living organisms by man and not an inherent quality of the organisms themselves.

As already mentioned, the animal kingdom is divided into four subkingdoms: the Protozoa, which are unicellular (or acellular) animals; the Mesozoa and Parazoa, which are two groups of multicellular animals not on the main line of evolutionary development; and the Metazoa, which contains the bulk of the multicellular groups.

Subkingdom Protozoa

PHYLUM PROTOZOA

Small organisms in which the body is not divided into cells. Some forms may be colonial, a colony consisting of a number of separate, complete individuals, which may however be linked by protoplasmic connections. The Protozoa are divided into four classes, mainly on the basis of their methods of locomotion.

CLASS MASTIGOPHORA (Flagellata)

Protozoa in which the main form of locomotion in the adult is by means of one or more flagella. Some species may also show amoeboid movement. The colonial habit is shown by some species. The class is split into two subclasses by virtue of their methods of nutrition.

SUBCLASS PHYTOMASTIGINA – Flagellates in which nutrition is holophytic, or which are obviously related to such forms. This group thus forms a link between the animal and plant kingdoms, and it is sometimes included in the plant kingdom. Most members of the subclass have not more than two flagella.

e.g. *Volvox, Ceratium, Dinobryon, Cryptomonas, Euglena, Vacuolaria.*

SUBCLASS ZOOMASTIGINA – Flagellates which do not contain chlorophyll, and are not similar in other respects to the Phytomastigina. A number of species are parasitic. Many species have more than two flagella. The systematic position of *Opalina* is open to debate; it is sometimes included in the class Ciliophora.

e.g. *Mastigamoeba, Multicilia, Trypanosoma, Trichomonas, Opalina.*

CLASS RHIZOPODA (Sarcodina)

Protozoa in which the main form of locomotion is by means of pseudopodia, which may be blunt (lobopodia), threadlike and often branching (filopodia), or thin and stiffened by a central filament (axopodia). Some species are parasitic. Some produce protective tests of various organic and mineral substances, such as the foraminiferans, the shells of which form the principal part of chalk and deep-sea ooze.

e.g. *Amoeba, Arcella, Polystomella, Globigerina, Heliosphaera, Dimorpha, Plasmodiophora.*

CLASS SPOROZOA

Protozoa in which there are usually no locomotory structures. Some, however, may show amoeboid or euglenoid movement. All are parasitic and produce large numbers of spores after syngamy. Many are serious pathogens in man and other animals.

SUBCLASS TELOSPORIDIA – The adult individual has a single nucleus.

e.g. *Monocystis, Eimeria, Plasmodium.*

SUBCLASS NEOSPORIDIA – The adult individual is a syncytium containing a number of nuclei.

e.g. *Myxobolus, Haplosporidium, Sarcocystis.*

CLASS CILIOPHORA

Protozoa which possess numerous cilia at some stage in the life cycle. Most species possess a meganucleus and micronucleus. This class contains some of the most intricately organized protozoans.

SUBCLASS CILIATA – The adults have cilia and do not have tentacles.

e.g. *Paramecium, Stentor, Euplotes, Vorticella.*

SUBCLASS SUCTORIA – The adults do not normally have cilia. Tentacles are present which have a suctorial function.

e.g. *Ephelota, Tokophyra.*

Subkingdom Mesozoa
PHYLUM MESOZOA

Minute animals in which the body consists of a single layer of ciliated cells enclosing a number of reproductive cells. The mesozoans are parasitic in invertebrates. Some authorities regard the mesozoans as being degenerate platyhelminths, others maintain that they have affinities with the protozoans, particularly with the Sporozoa.

e.g. *Rhopalura, Dicyemennea.*

Subkingdom Parazoa
PHYLUM PORIFERA – the sponges

Sessile, aquatic organisms, primitively vase-shaped, although few remain so throughout life. The body wall has two cellular layers: an outer layer of epithelial-like cells, and an inner layer of flagellate choanocyte cells. Between these two layers is a jelly containing scattered cells, many of which are involved in the production of spicules which form supporting material. Numerous ostia, through which water passes into the body cavity or paragaster, and one or more oscula, through which water passes out, are present. One family of sponges occurs in fresh water, the remainder are marine.

CLASS CALCAREA

Sponges which have a skeleton of calcareous spicules.

e.g. *Sycon, Grantia, Leucosolenia.*

CLASS HEXACTINELLIDA

Sponges with a skeleton of six-rayed spicules composed of silica.

e.g. *Euplectella.*

CLASS DEMOSPONGIAE

The skeleton may be composed of silica, or spongin (horny protein material), or both. The spicules are never six-rayed.

e.g. *Cliona, Halichondria, Euspongia.*

Subkingdom Metazoa

The remainder of the animal kingdom is contained within the subkingdom Metazoa. The organisms are multi-cellular, the cells being arranged into tissues and, excepting the first two phyla, the tissues are arranged into organs, which in turn form organ-systems. The first two phyla are diploblastic and basically radially symmetrical. They are often amalgamated to form a single phylum, Coelenterata, with the two phyla below ranked as subphyla.

PHYLUM CNIDARIA

Basically radially symmetrical, sedentary or free-swimming aquatic animals, the majority of which are marine, although some hydrozoans are found in fresh water. The body wall consists of two cellular layers, the ectoderm and endoderm, separated by a non-cellular mesoglea. The body is sac-like, the cavity being the coelenteron which has a single opening surrounded by tentacles. The cnidarians can be distinguished from the ctenophores by the following three characteristics: a) typically two types of individual occur during the life cycle, the polyp, a sedentary phase, and the medusa, a free-swimming phase; b) movement is by muscular action as opposed to ciliary action in the ctenophores; c) cells known as cnidoblasts are present which contain an eversible thread used for stinging and capturing prey. The nervous system consists of nerve nets throughout the body, and various sensory structures.

CLASS HYDROZOA

Cnidarians in which the coelenteron is a simple undivided cavity. The gonads develop in the ectoderm. Typically, the polyp phase is a colony of polymorphic individuals, covered by a chitinous perisarc secreted by the ectoderm, and both the polyp and medusa phases are present in the life cycle. The medusa typically has a velum, an extension of the edge of the medusa forming a shelf-like membrane projecting inwards. In some the medusa phase is absent, in some the polyp is much reduced. Some species form pelagic colonies of polyps.

e.g. *Hydra, Obelia, Millepora, Physalia.*

CLASS SCYPHOZOA – the true jellyfish

The coelenteron is typically divided into four pouches, and has gastric filaments, small internal tentacles concerned with enzyme secretion. Symmetry is typically tetramerous. The gonads are endodermal. The mesoglea contains cells and fibres. The medusa is without a velum, but has a scalloped margin. The adults are typically the medusa stage. In a few species, the free-swimming phase is absent and the adult is a sessile polyp, which is, however, similar to the larval stage of more typical scyphozoans. The larval form of typical species is a polyp-like scyphistoma, which, by repeated budding (strobilation), produces a number of ephyra larvae that subsequently develop into adult jelly-fish.

e.g. *Haliclystus, Carybdea, Aurelia, Rhizostoma.*

CLASS ANTHOZOA – the sea anemones and corals
The coelenteron is septate. The gonads are endodermal.
The mesoglea contains fibrous material. All species are
sessile polyps, the medusoid stage being absent. Some
species are solitary and without skeletal material (sea
anemones), but many species form internal or external
skeletons (corals). Many of the corals are colonial.

SUBCLASS ALCYONARIA (Octocorallia) – Anthozoa with
eight septa and eight pinnate tentacles.
  e.g. *Alcyonium.*

SUBCLASS ZOANTHARIA (Hexacorallia) – The number of
septa and tentacles, which are simple, is six, or a multiple
thereof.
  e.g. *Actinia, Metridium, Madrepora.*

PHYLUM CTENOPHORA – the comb-jellies
Typically radially symmetrical animals with transparent,
often globular, sac-like bodes. Locomotion is brought
about by numerous cilia which are arranged to form eight
longitudinal comb-plates. Cnidoblasts are absent, although
lassoo cells, or colloblasts, are present. These are modified
epidermal cells with an adhesive function. The ctenophores are not directly comparable to either polyp or
medusa forms, although they obviously have affinities with
the cnidarians.

CLASS TENTACULATA
Ctenophores bearing long tentacles.
  e.g. *Pleurobrachia, Cestum.*

CLASS NUDA
Ctenophores without tentacles. There is only one known
living genus in this class.
  Beroe.

THE CLASSIFICATION OF ANIMALS

The remaining phyla of the animal kingdom consist of triploblastic animals which are basically bilaterally symmetrical, although in some groups secondary radial symmetry is shown. The body is at the organ-system level of organization. The first two phyla can be grouped as the Acoelomata. The spaces between the organs are filled with somewhat undifferentiated parenchymatous material.

PHYLUM PLATYHELMINTHES – the flatworms

Typically dorso-ventrally flattened. A gut is present (except in the Cestoda) but there is no anus, the only opening being the mouth which is mid-ventral or antero-ventral in position. The excretory system consists of flame-bulbs (cup-shaped, ciliated cells) connected by excretory canals. The nervous system consists basically of a nerve net with an anterior concentration of nerve cells and a number of longitudinal nerve cords. There is no circulatory system. The reproductive system is complex. Most species are hermaphrodite. In the parasitic species the life cycle is complex and often involves more than one host. The platyhelminths occur in marine, fresh water, terrestrial, and parasitic habitats.

CLASS TURBELLARIA – the planarians

Free-living flatworms. The epidermis is cellular or syncytial and contains rhabdites—rod-like structures secreted by glandular cells. The epidermis is usually ciliated.

e.g. *Dalyellia, Planaria, Convoluta.*

CLASS TREMATODA – the flukes

Parasitic flatworms. The body is without an epidermis and not ciliated, but covered with a cuticle, often with spines. Suckers are present for attachment to the host.

SUBCLASS MONOGENEA (Heterocotylea) – Mainly ecto-parasitic on aquatic vertebrates, with only one host in the life cycle. Typically with a posterior sucker which may be subdivided, and an anterior adhesive organ.

e.g. *Polystomum, Octobothrium, Gyrodactylus.*

SUBCLASS DIGENEA (Malacocotylea) – Endoparasitic, the adults usually occurring in the intestine, blood, or body cavities of vertebrates. There is usually more than one host during the life cycle. Anterior and ventral suckers are usually present, the anterior sucker surrounding the mouth.

e.g. *Fasciola, Schistosoma, Diplostomum.*

SUBCLASS ASPIDOGASTREA – Mainly endoparasitic in aquatic hosts, invertebrate and vertebrate. An extensive ventral sucker-plate is present, consisting of many individual suckers.

e.g. *Aspidogaster.*

CLASS CESTODA – the tapeworms
Endoparasitic in the alimentary canals of vertebrates. Like the trematodes, the epidermis is absent and the body is covered by a cuticle. There is no alimentary system.

SUBCLASS CESTODARIA (Monozoa) – A small group of primitive cestodes which resemble trematodes in many respects, but are included in the Cestoda principally because of the lack of a gut. They have a small sucker at the 'posterior' end, and a frilled attachment rosette at the 'anterior' end. They are parasitic in the gut of fish, principally elasmobranchs.

e.g. *Gyrocotyle.*

SUBCLASS EUCESTODA (Merozoa) – 'Typical' tapeworms in which the body consists of a tape (strobila) made up of proglottides formed continuously a little behind the anterior end, those the furthest from the anterior end thus being the oldest. Each proglottis, when mature, contains a complete reproductive system. The anterior end of the body is specialized as a scolex bearing hooks and suckers for attachment to the wall of the gut of the host.

e.g. *Taenia, Diphyllobothrium.*

PHYLUM NEMERTEA (Rhynchocoela) – the proboscis worms

Elongated, slightly flattened animals with a ciliated ectoderm and lacking a cuticle. The alimentary canal is complete, i.e. both mouth and anus are present. An eversible proboscis is present, dorsal to the anterior part of the alimentary canal. The excretory system is of the flame-cell type. A blood vascular system is present. The sexes are separate. The gonads are repeated along the length of the body. Principally marine animals, although some occur in fresh water and a few are terrestrial.

CLASS ANOPLA

The 'brain' is anterior to the position of the mouth. The proboscis is unarmed.

e.g. *Lineus, Carinoma.*

CLASS ENOPLA

The 'brain' is posterior to the position of the mouth. The proboscis is usually armed with spines.

e.g. *Malacobdella, Amphiporus.*

The following three phyla may be grouped together as

the Pseudocoelomata. In these the region between the ectoderm and endoderm is not filled completely with mesodermal material as in the Acoelomata, but has fluid-filled spaces. These spaces are not lined totally with mesoderm and thus form not a true coelom, but a pseudo-coel. Excretory systems, where present, are typically based on the flame-cell type. Circulatory and respiratory systems are absent.

PHYLUM ACANTHOCEPHALA – the spiny-headed worms

Usually small, elongate animals, parasitic in vertebrate intestines, with arthropods as intermediate hosts. The anterior end of the body bears an eversible, spiny proboscis. There is no alimentary canal. A flame-cell excretory system is present in primitive forms only. The body is covered by a thin cuticle, often with spines. The sexes are separate.

e.g. *Neoechinorhynchus, Corynosoma.*

PHYLUM ASCHELMINTHES

This phylum contains six groups of animals of uncertain taxonomic relationships. These six groups are here ranked as classes, although some authorities upgrade these classes to the rank of phyla. The animals in these groups are all more or less worm-like in appearance. They have a complete alimentary canal, usually with a well-developed pharynx. The body is covered by a cuticle.

CLASS ROTIFERA

Minute aquatic animals. Typically, the pharynx has jaws and a ciliated 'wheel-organ' is present. This is used for feeding and locomotion. The posterior end often has a jointed tail for temporary attachment to the substratum. The excretory system consists of flame-cells, and a pair of nephridial tubules. The sexes are separate, and in most species the male is degenerate in structure.

e.g. *Notops, Gastropus, Melicerta.*

CLASS GASTROTRICHA

Minute aquatic animals. The pharynx is a muscular tube. The ventral surface of the body is ciliated, the cilia often being arranged in longitudinal bands. The posterior end of the body has adhesive organs. The dorsal surface bears bristles or scales. Excretory systems are present in only a few species. Typically hermaphroditic but in some the male system is degenerate and reproduction is by parthenogenesis.

e.g. *Macrodasys, Chaetonotus.*

CLASS KINORHYNCHA (Echinodera)

Minute marine animals. The body is externally segmented into fourteen metameres. The first of these is the head which bears oral spines and is retractable. The cuticle forms one dorsal and two ventral plates on each metamere. Cilia are absent but spines are present. The posterior end has a pair of adhesive glands. The excretory system consists of a pair of protonephridial flame-bulbs.

e.g. *Kinorhyncha, Echinoderella.*

CLASS PRIAPULIDA

A small group of marine animals which may reach a length of 100mm. The body consists of a cylindrical trunk, which is annulated, and a globular, invaginable proboscis bearing rows of papillae, and oral spines. The posterior end of the body bears numerous caudal appendages. The priapulids differ from other aschelminths in that the excretory system is composed of flagellate solenocytes, and not of ciliate flame-bulbs.

e.g. *Priapulus, Halicryptus.*

CLASS NEMATODA – the roundworms

Free-living and parasitic animals, typically with elongated, cylindrical bodies, pointed at both ends. The epidermis is thickened internally forming four chords along the length of the body, one dorsal, one ventral, and two lateral. The body is covered by a thick cuticle which may bear scales, spines, or papillae. Cilia are absent from all parts of the body. The anterior end may have structures for attachment in the parasitic species. The excretory system consists of two intracellular tubes in the lateral chords. The alimentary canal is a straight tube. The nematodes possess characteristic muscle cells with inwardly pointing non-contractile processes. The sexes are usually separate.

e.g. *Ascaris, Rhabditis, Strongylus.*

CLASS NEMATOMORPHA – the hairworms

Similar in appearance to nematodes but greatly elongated. Epidermal chords are absent. Excretory system absent. The alimentary canal is to some extent degenerate. The body cavity may be filled with parenchymatous cells. The adults are free-living, the young stages are parasitic in insects.

e.g. *Gordius, Parachordodes.*

PHYLUM ENTOPROCTA

The entoprocts differ from other pseudocoelomate groups in that the body is not worm-like, but is a sessile, stalked polyp. The alimentary canal is recurved such that both mouth and anus are uppermost. The mouth and anus are surrounded by a single circlet of ciliated tentacles. The pseudocoel tends to be filled with parenchymatous material. The excretory system consists of a pair of protonephridia with flame-bulbs. Development is via a characteristic, somewhat trochosphere-like larva. The adults may be solitary or colonial, and, although the individual animals are small, extensive colonies may be formed encrusting stones, etc. All but one genus, which occurs in fresh water, are marine.

e.g. *Pedicellina, Loxosoma.*

The remaining thirteen phyla of the animal kingdom can be grouped as the Coelomata. In these animals, the body possesses a true coelom since it is lined completely by mesodermal material. The Coelomata can be divided into the protostomial and deuterostomial groups with regard to the embryonic position of the mouth, and to the mode of cleavage of the egg. The first eight coelomate phyla are protostomial, and of these the first three are lophophorate, possessing a lophophore surrounding the mouth. In this respect they bear a resemblance to the Entoprocta. The latter, however, differ in that the ring of ciliated tentacles surrounds both the mouth and the anus, and the animals do not possess a true coelom. The three lophophorate phyla consist of aquatic animals, mainly marine, although the phylum Ectoprocta also has fresh water members. Segmentation is not shown in any of these phyla. The animals are more or less sedentary in the adult stage, with free-swimming larval forms.

PHYLUM PHORONIDA

Typically small, polyp-like, tube-dwelling organisms, with a horseshoe-shaped lophophore. The alimentary canal is U-shaped, but as in all lophophorates the anus is outside the lophophore. A small lobe, the epistome, is present between the mouth and the anus. A vascular system is present with blood containing haemoglobin. Two excretory organs are present. The animals are hermaphrodite. Development is via a free-swimming actinotroch larva of the trochosphere type.

e.g. *Phoronis*.

PHYLUM ECTOPROCTA

Sedentary, and usually colonial, polyp-like animals, in which the body typically consists of a body wall (zooecium) and internal organs (polypide). Periodically, the polypide degenerates within the zooecium forming a small mass, the brown body. A new polypide reforms within the zooecium and the brown body is expelled. Ectoprocts have no excretory or vascular systems. They are hermaphrodite, and typically have free-swimming larvae of the trochosphere type. Asexual reproduction occurs by budding. Polymorphism is common. Two extreme polymorphic forms are the bristle-like vibracula used for wafting sediment away from the colony, and the avicularia (so called due to their resemblance to a bird's head) used especially for trapping passing larvae of encrusting organisms.

CLASS PHYLACTOLAEMATA

Fresh-water forms, in which the lophophore is horseshoe-shaped. An epistome is present.

e.g. *Plumatella*.

CLASS GYMNOLAEMATA

Mainly marine types, with a circular lophophore. There is no epistome.

e.g. *Crista, Bugula, Flustra, Alcyonidium*.

PHYLUM BRACHIOPODA – the lamp-shells

Marine lophophorates characterized by the possession of a bivalved shell. The two shell valves are in dorsal and ventral positions (cf. bivalved molluscs in which the valves are lateral). A stalk, or peduncle, for attachment to the substratum, is typically present. The peduncle passes either through an aperture in the posterior region of the larger ventral valve, or between the valves. The lophophore is a complex ciliated structure, and in some forms it is strengthened by skeletal processes from the dorsal valve. A pair of excretory organs is present. A vascular system is present, consisting of a dorsal vessel with a number of blindly ending anterior and posterior vessels. The sexes are usually separate. Development is via a free-swimming larva.

CLASS INARTICULATA (Ecardines)
Brachiopods in which the two valves of the shell are not hinged. The shell consists mainly of chitinous material and calcium phosphate. The lophophore is without skeletal structures.

e.g. *Lingula, Crania.*

CLASS ARTICULATA (Testicardines)
Brachiopods with hinged valves. The shell is made up principally of calcium carbonate particles. The lophophore typically has skeletal structures. The alimentary canal has no anus.

e.g. *Terebratella, Gryphus.*

The following five phyla consist of the non-lophophorate protostomes. The first two of these are small groups of doubtful affinities, sometimes included in the phylum Annelida. The remaining three phyla are large groups, the phylum Arthropoda being the largest phylum of the animal kingdom with respect to the number of species.

54

PHYLUM SIPUNCULIDA

The sipunculids are cylindrical, elongate worm-like animals. They are sedentary, burrowing, marine forms. The mouth is surrounded by lobes or tentacles, and the anterior region of the body is invaginable. The anus is dorsal and somewhat anterior in position. The excretory system consists of a pair of nephridia. The nervous system is annelid-like, but shows no sign of segmentation. The sexes are separate. Development is via larvae of a modified trochosphere type.

e.g. *Sipunculus, Golfingia.*

PHYLUM ECHIUROIDEA

Burrowing, marine animals, with a cylindrical or ovoid body, unsegmented in the adult although the larvae show traces of segmentation. Anterior to the mouth, a prostomium is present which may be elongated to form a proboscis. A pair of ventral chaetae is present, and in some a number of posterior chaetae are also present. The nervous system is annelid-like, but unsegmented in the adult. The sexes are separate and in some there is extreme sexual dimorphism. Development is via a trochosphere-type larva.

e.g. *Bonellia, Echiurus.*

PHYLUM MOLLUSCA

Molluscs, with the possible exception of some amphineurans (see below), are unsegmented. The body typically consists of a head, often well developed, a ventral, muscular foot, and a dorsal visceral hump in which are housed most of the organs of the body. The visceral hump is covered by a thin layer of tissue, the mantle, which typically secretes a principally calcareous shell. The mantle is extended at its edges into flaps which enclose a mantle cavity. The anus and excretory ducts open into this cavity, which also typically contains gills, or ctenidia. A large digestive gland (hepatopancreas) is present leading from the stomach. The vascular system consists of a three-chambered heart (except in one group of prosobranch gastropods in which only two chambers are present), a number of vessels, and often a haemocoel. The true coelom may be restricted to the pericardial cavity, the gonads, and the kidneys. Development is typically via a trochosphere-type larva. Most molluscs are aquatic, in both marine and fresh-water habitats. A number are terrestrial.

CLASS AMPHINEURA (Loricata)

Somewhat elongated molluscs with the mouth and anus at opposite ends of the body. Eyes are absent. The mantle covers the whole of the dorsal surface and contains calcareous spicules, which may be condensed to form one or more plates. The nervous system is without ganglia. A chitinous strap bearing teeth (the radula) is typically present on the floor of the buccal cavity. All are marine. The three subclasses below are sometimes ranked as separate classes; sometimes only the first is thus separated.

SUBCLASS MONOPLACOPHORA – Amphineurans with a single-plate covering the dorsal surface. The head bears a pair of small tentacles, a pair of branched sensory tufts, and a pair of labial palps. A number of features of mono-placophorans appear to be segmental. There are several paired ostia, six pairs of excretory organs, two pairs of gonads, five pairs of ctenidia, and eight pairs of shell muscles. Habitat is the ocean depths.

e.g. *Neopilina*.

SUBCLASS POLYPLACOPHORA – Shore-living forms with eight overlapping shell-plates. Tentacles are absent. The foot is large. The gills form two rows, one on either side of the body.

    e.g. *Lepidopleurus, Chiton.*

SUBCLASS APLACOPHORA – Elongate, worm-like forms in which the foot is reduced or absent. The mantle secretes spicules but these do not combine to form plates. Gills may be absent. Some are without a radula.

    e.g. *Neomenia, Chaetoderma.*

CLASS GASTROPODA

Molluscs with a well-developed head bearing tentacles and eyes, a large flat foot, and a visceral hump which is twisted (torsion), basically through 180°, such that the primitively posterior mantle cavity becomes anterior in position. The gills and anus are then anterior in position, the heart is rotated, and the visceral loop of the nervous system becomes twisted. The visceral hump is also typically coiled and with a single shell. Ganglia are present in the nervous system. A radula is present. Development is typically via trochosphere and veliger larvae, or it may be direct.

SUBCLASS PROSOBRANCHIA – Mainly marine forms with full (180°) torsion. The head has one pair of tentacles. Almost all with shell, which is cap-like (limpets) or coiled. In forms with a coiled shell, an operculum is typically present. The sexes are usually separate.

    e.g. *Patella, Trochus, Littorina, Cypraea, Buccinum, Murex, Conus.*

SUBCLASS OPISTHOBRANCHIA – Mostly marine forms which show detorsion through 90° or 180°. The shell is typically reduced, internal, or absent. The head bears two pairs of tentacles. The gills may be reduced, respiratory exchange occurring through accessory structures or the general body surface. Most forms are hermaphrodite.

   e.g. *Actaeon, Aplysia, Clione, Doris, Eolis.*

SUBCLASS PULMONATA – Fresh-water and terrestrial forms which show full torsion. Typically with a shell, but without an operculum. Reduction of the shell occurs in the slugs. Gills are absent and the mantle cavity is a lung for air breathing. The head bears two pairs of tentacles. Development is direct, without larvae.

   e.g. *Limnaea, Ancylus, Helix, Limax.*

CLASS SCAPHOPODA
Molluscs with an elongate, tapered, tubular shell, open at both ends. The foot is reduced. A number of prehensile tentacles are present. A radula is present. Gills are absent, respiratory exchange occurring through the mantle cavity lining. Development is via trochosphere and veliger larvae.

   e.g. *Dentalium.*

CLASS BIVALVIA (Lamellibranchiata, Pelecypoda)
Laterally compressed molluscs with a shell consisting of two valves, joined dorsally by a ligament, and usually hinged. Tentacles, eyes, and radula are absent. Labial palps are present. Two longitudinal ctenidia are present, each consisting typically of two rows of ciliated gill filaments. The sexes are usually separate. Development is via trochosphere and veliger larvae in marine forms, and via glochidia larvae in fresh-water types. The class is divided into three (or four) subclasses on the basis of gill structure.

SUBCLASS PROTOBRANCHIA – The ctenidia consist of flat gill filaments, and are used for respiration only.

e.g. *Nucula, Yoldia.*

SUBCLASS LAMELLIBRANCHIA – The gill filaments are reflected such that each ctenidium is W-shaped in cross section. The ctenidia are used for filter-feeding, as well as for respiration. This subclass may be divided into two subclasses: Filibranchia, in which the gill filaments have ciliary connections only, and Eulamellibranchia, in which tissue connections are present in the ctenidia.

e.g. *Anomia, Mytilus, Pecten, Cardium, Ostrea, Anodonta, Teredo.*

SUBCLASS SEPTIBRANCHIA – The ctenidia are modified, forming perforated muscular septa which act as diaphragms for drawing water into the mantle cavity.

e.g. *Cuspidaria.*

CLASS CEPHALOPODA (Siphonopoda)
Highly developed molluscs, elongated in a dorsal direction. The head is surrounded by tentacles. Eyes are present. The nervous system is highly developed. The foot is represented by a siphon, used for rapid expulsion of water from the mantle cavity. Development is usually direct. All species are marine.

SUBCLASS TETRABRANCHIATA – Cephalopods with chambered shell, the animal living in the terminal chamber. There are numerous tentacles. The eyes are simple. The siphon is double. There are two pairs of gills.

e.g. *Nautilus.*

SUBCLASS DIBRANCHIATA—Cephalopods with the shell internal or absent (except *Argonauta,* the female of which produces an external, paper-like shell). There are eight or ten tentacles, bearing suckers. The eyes are highly developed. The siphon is single. There is one pair of gills. Pelagic or semi-sedentary.

e.g. *Sepia, Loligo, Octopus, Argonauta.*

PHYLUM ANNELIDA – the segmented worms
Typically metamerically segmented, coelomate worms, with only one segment anterior to the mouth. The body wall contains an outer layer of circular muscles, and an inner layer of longitudinal muscles. The body is typically covered with a cuticle secreted by the epidermis. Chitinous chaetae are usually present. The excretory system consists of nephridia or coelomoducts, or both. The nervous system consists of a double ventral nerve cord with segmental ganglia, and a pair of ganglia dorsal to the pharynx connected to the ventral nerve cord by circum-pharyngeal commissures. Larvae are trochospheres.

CLASS POLYCHAETA
Mainly marine annelids with well-developed segmentation and head with jaws and eyes. Each trunk segment typically has lateral outgrowths (parapodia) which bear numerous chaetae. The sexes are usually separate. The polychaetes are often divided into two groups: Errantia, which are free-swimming, and Sedentaria, which can be further divided into tube-forming and burrowing types. The tubicolous forms often have modified tentacles forming a fan-like structure for feeding at the anterior end. The division into Errantia and Sedentaria is based, not on evolutionary considerations, but on ecological criteria.

e.g. Errantia: *Nereis, Eunice, Eulalia, Aphrodite.*

Sedentaria: *Chaetopterus, Pomatoceros, Sabella, Arenicola.*

CLASS MYSOSTOMARIA

External or internal parasites of echinoderms. The body is disc-shaped, with five pairs of parapodia bearing hooked chaetae, and four pairs of suckers. They are hermaphrodite. The mysostomarians are included in the phylum Annelida as they develop via polychaete-like, free-swimming trochosphere larvae, and are considered by some to be degenerate polychaetes.

e.g. *Mysostoma.*

CLASS ARCHIANNELIDA

Small simplified annelids, usually without chaetae and parapodia. Segmentation is reduced. They are thought to have evolved from polychaete stock by reduction of structure and retention of larval characteristics in that the epidermis is ciliated and the nervous system remains attached to it.

e.g. *Polygordius, Dinophilus.*

CLASS OLIGOCHAETA

Terrestrial and fresh-water annelids with reduced external features. Parapodia are absent. Chaetae are reduced. The head is usually without appendages. All are hermaphrodite, but cross-fertilization is usual. Development is direct, without larval stages. The oligochaetes can be divided into two ecological groups:

Megadrili – large terrestrial forms.

e.g. *Lumbricus, Allolobophora.*

Microdrili – small fresh-water forms.

e.g. *Tubifex, Stylaria.*

CLASS HIRUDINEA – the leeches

Marine, fresh-water, and terrestrial annelids. The body is flattened, and consists of a prostomium and usually thirty-three other segments, each of which is subdivided by a number of annuli. With the exception of the genus *Acanthobdella,* chaetae are absent. Anterior and posterior suckers are present. The coelom is reduced, and filled with mesenchyme cells except for a number of longitudinal sinuses. The leeches are carnivorous or blood-sucking animals. They are cross-fertilizing hermaphrodites.

e.g. *Acanthobdella, Glossiphonia, Hirudo, Haemopsis.*

PHYLUM ARTHROPODA

The largest phylum, with more species than all other phyla combined. The arthropods are segmented with a chitinous exoskeleton, which is generally relatively hard, but is flexible between segments and at the joints of the typically jointed appendages. The paired appendages occur on some or all segments, and at least one pair function as jaws. Periodically during growth, the hard exoskeleton is shed (ecdysis), a new, initially soft cuticle having been secreted below the old cuticle. The coelom is reduced, and is replaced by the haemocoel of the open blood system. The nervous system is similar in basic organization to that of annelids. Excretory systems are varied, but do not consist of nephridia. Patterns of development are varied. Cilia are absent, except in the class Onychophora.

CLASS ONYCHOPHORA

Animals which in many respects appear intermediate between annelids and arthropods, and are sometimes put in a separate phylum. The body is elongate and uniform in structure. The cuticle is thin and soft. Segmentation is not well shown externally, except for the paired appendages. The head consists of three segments, bearing preantennae, jaws and papillae respectively. Simple eyes are present. The trunk is of 17 to 43 segments, each of which bears a pair of appendages resembling parapodia, but bearing claws. Tracheae are present. Cilia are present in the genital organs. Development is direct. Occur in damp situations on land in the tropics.

e.g. *Peripatus*.

CLASS PAUROPODA

Minute arthropods with eleven or twelve segments posterior to the head, bearing ten pairs of appendages, nine of which are locomotory. The head bears mandibles and branched antennae. The body segments tend to be fused in pairs dorsally. Five pairs of long setae are present on the sides of the body. Setae are also present on the limbs. Tracheae and eyes are absent. The gonopores are on the third trunk segment. Development is via larvae, initially with three pairs of legs. Four moults occur before the adult form is attained. Occur in damp situations on land.

e.g. *Pauropus*.

CLASS DIPLOPODA – the millipedes

Elongate, tracheate arthropods, with numerous segments. The head typically bears one pair each of antennae, mandibles, and maxillae. The first four segments of the trunk are single, each with one pair of legs. The remainder are typically fused in pairs, each apparent 'segment' bearing two pairs of legs. Simple eyes are present. Gonopores occur on the third segment of the trunk. The young hatch with three pairs of legs. Terrestrial and herbivorous.

SUBCLASS PSELAPHOGNATHA – Minute forms with a soft cuticle, and with numerous bristles. The trunk

has eleven segments, the last two of which are leg-less.

e.g. *Polyxenus.*

SUBCLASS CHILOGNATHA – 'Typical' millipedes with a hard cuticle. In the male, one pair of legs is modified for use during mating.

e.g. *Glomeris, Polydesmus, Julus, Platydesmus.*

CLASS CHILOPODA – the centipedes
Elongate, tracheate arthropods. The head bears one pair of antennae, one pair of mandibles, and two pairs of maxillae. The trunk segments are not fused. Fifteen or more pairs of walking legs are present. A pair of poison claws are present on the first trunk segment. Eyes, if present, may be simple or compound. Gonopores occur at the posterior end of the body. Terrestrial and carnivorous forms.

UBCLASS EPIMORPHA – The young hatch with the full complement of segments and legs.

e.g. *Geophilus, Scolopendra.*

SUBCLASS ANAMORPHA – The young hatch with seven pairs of legs, and acquire further segments and legs during juvenile moults.

e.g. *Lithobius, Scutigera.*

CLASS SYMPHYLA
Small, terrestrial, tracheate arthropods, with sixteen pairs of appendages in the adult, twelve of which are loco-motory. The antennae are long with many segments. The posterior segment of the body bears a pair of tail-like appendages. Spinning glands and spinnerets are present. The gonopores are on the third trunk segment. Newly

hatched larvae have six or seven pairs of legs and go through six larval stages before attaining adult structure.

e.g. *Scutigerella.*

CLASS INSECTA

Tracheate arthropods, with the body divided into three regions. The head (six fused segments) bears a pair each of antennae, mandibles, and maxillae, and a labium formed of fused second maxillae. The thorax (three segments) bears three pairs of legs, and typically two pairs of wings. The abdomen (eleven segments) is without locomotory appendages in the adult, except in the Apterygota, some species of which have rudimentary limbs. External genitalia are typically present, developed from abdominal appendages. Paired cerci are often present at the tip of the abdomen. Compound eyes are typically present. The insects show considerable diversity of form and habit.

SUBCLASS APTERYGOTA (Ametabola) – Primitively wingless insects, with rudiments of locomotory appendages on the abdomen. Metamorphosis is slight or absent.

Order Protura: e.g. *Acerentomon.*
Order Diplura: e.g. *Campodea.*
Order Thysanura (bristle-tails): e.g. *Lepisma, Petrobius.*
Order Collembola (spring-tails): e.g. *Lipura, Sminthurus.*

SUBCLASS PTERYGOTA (Metabola) – Winged insects, although some have secondarily adopted a wingless form. Metamorphosis of some type is present. The further classification of pterygote insects is too complex to be dealt with fully, and thus the simplest system is here adopted.

DIVISION EXOPTERYGOTA (Hemimetabola) – Insects with simple metamorphosis. The larvae are nymphs, resembling the adult form in basic structure, but wingless. Wing growth is external.

Order Ephemeroptera (may-flies): e.g. *Ephemera*.

Order Odonata (dragon- and damsel-flies): e.g. *Agrion, Aeshna*.

Order Dictyoptera (cockroaches and mantids): e.g. *Periplaneta, Mantis*.

Order Isoptera (termites): e.g. *Mastotermes*.

Order Zoraptera: e.g. *Zorotypus*.

Order Plecoptera (stone-flies): e.g. *Perla*.

Order Grylloblattodea: e.g. *Grylloblatta*.

Order Phasmida (leaf- and stick-insects): e.g. *Carausius, Phyllium*.

Order Orthoptera (grasshoppers, locusts and crickets): e.g. *Tettigonia, Acheta, Locusta*.

Order Embioptera (web-spinners): e.g. *Embia*.

Order Dermaptera (earwigs): e.g. *Forficula*.

Order Psocoptera (bark- and book-lice): e.g. *Psocus*.

Order Mallophaga (biting-lice): e.g. *Menopon*.

Order Siphunculata (Anoplura) (sucking-lice): e.g. *Phthirus, Pediculus*.

Order Thysanoptera (thrips): e.g. *Thrips*.

Order Hemiptera (bugs): e.g. *Magicicada, Aphis, Coccus, Cimex, Rhodnius, Corixa*.

DIVISION ENDOPTERYGOTA (Holometabola) – Larvae are specialized, and do not resemble adults. Metamorphosis is complex, involving pupal stage. Wing growth is internal.

Order Neuroptera (lacewings and antlions): e.g. *Sialis, Chrysopa*.

Order Coleoptera (beetles): e.g. *Carabus, Cupes,*

Dytiscus, Lacanus, Tenebrio, Coccinella.
Order Strepsiptera (stylopids): e.g. *Stylops.*
Order Mecoptera (scorpion-flies): e.g. *Panorpa.*
Order Trichoptera (caddis-flies): e.g. *Phryganea.*
Order Zeugloptera: e.g. *Micropteryx.*
Order Lepidoptera: (butterflies and moths):
　　e.g. *Hepialus, Sphinx, Tinea, Papilio, Pieris, Bombyx.*
Order Diptera (true flies): e.g. *Tipula, Culex, Chironomus, Tabanus, Drosophila, Musca, Glossina.*
Order Siphonaptera (fleas): e.g. *Pulex.*
Order Hymenoptera (ants, bees, wasps, sawflies):
　　e.g. *Nematus, Ichneumon, Formica, Vespula, Bombus, Apis.*

CLASS CRUSTACEA

Principally aquatic, non-tracheate arthropods. The body consists of a head of six segments, and a trunk divisible into thorax and abdomen, the abdomen being defined as that part of the trunk posterior to the most posterior gonopore. The head bears two pairs of antennae (or antennules and antennae), and one pair each of mandibles, maxillules (first maxillae), and maxillae (second maxillae). The class is large and considerable variety of form is shown by its members. The thoracic region usually bears at least four pairs of appendages. The abdomen may or may not bear appendages. The limbs are either of a usually narrow stenopodial type, or of a usually broad and flat phyllopodial type. Many forms have a dorsal carapace covering part or all of the body. The end of the abdomen usually bears a non-segmental telson. Compound eyes are usually present. Respiratory exchange is generally via gills. Development is varied, but usually includes a nauplius larva.

SUBCLASS BRANCHIOPODA – Mainly fresh-water types, with more than four pairs of limbs of the phyllopodial type. A carapace is often present.

e.g. *Chirocephalus, Apus, Daphnia.*

SUBCLASS CEPHALOCARIDA – Marine forms with a thorax of ten segments, each with a pair of stenopodial limbs. The abdomen is without appendages.

e.g. *Hutchinsoniella.*

SUBCLASS OSTRACODA – Marine and fresh-water forms, with not more than two pairs of trunk limbs, which are of the stenopodial type. A bivalved carapace is present. Locomotion is brought about by the use of the antennae.

e.g. *Cypris.*

SUBCLASS COPEPODA – Marine and fresh-water forms, many of which are parasitic, without compound eyes or carapace. Usually with six pairs of thoracic limbs, and without abdominal limbs.

e.g. *Calanus, Cyclops, Notodelphys, Lernaea, Herpyllobius.*

SUBCLASS MYSTACOCARIDA – Marine forms retaining many larval characteristics. The thorax has five pairs of appendages, of which four are reduced. The abdomen is without appendages. Compound eyes are absent.

e.g. *Derocheilocaris.*

SUBCLASS BRANCHIURA – Marine and fresh-water forms, which are temporary parasites on fish. The body is flattened and disc-shaped. The abdomen is unsegmented and without appendages. The second maxillae are modified to form suckers.

e.g. *Argulus.*

SUBCLASS CIRRIPEDIA (barnacles) – Marine, sessile, highly modified forms. The carapace encloses the whole body, and often forms calcareous plates. Antennae and compound eyes are absent. The thorax typically has six pairs of limbs. The abdomen is reduced. The life cycle typically includes free-swimming nauplius larvae. These develop into bivalved cyprid larvae. The antennules of these larvae have, at their bases, cement glands used for attachment to the substratum prior to development into the adult form. Some are parasitic, mainly on higher crustaceans, and are reduced further, being without appendages or segmentation in the adult. Some of these cause parasitic castration of the host. Although these parasitic forms, in the adult stage, show virtually no crustacean characteristics, their life cycles include typically crustacean free-swimming larvae.

    e.g. *Lepas, Balanus, Sacculina, Synagoga.*

SUBCLASS MALACOSTRACA – Mainly aquatic forms, with eight thoracic segments, and usually six abdominal segments, typically all bearing appendages. A thoracic carapace is present in many. Compound eyes, usually stalked, are present. The head is usually well developed.

Superorder Leptostraca: e.g. *Nebalia.*
Superorder Syncarida: e.g. *Anaspides.*
Superorder Hoplocarida: e.g. *Squilla.*
Superorder Peracarida: e.g. *Mysis, Diastylis, Tanais, Ligia, Oniscus, Talitrus, Gammarus.*
Superorder Pancarida: e.g. *Thermosbaena.*
Superorder Eucarida: e.g. *Euphausia, Palaemon, Crangon, Astacus, Carcinus, Eupagurus, Uca.*

CLASS MEROSTOMATA (Xiphosurida)

Primitive marine arthropods. The heavily built body consists of a cephalothorax, basically of eight segments, covered by a horseshoe-shaped carapace, hinged to an abdomen of six fused segments. The cephalothorax bears one pair of chelicerae, one pair of pedipalps similar to walking legs, four pairs of walking legs, and a pair of chilaria, representing rudimentary appendages. Compound eyes are present. The abdomen bears six pairs of appendages, the first of which is fused to form a genital operculum, on which are the gonopores. The remaining five pairs bear numerous gill filaments forming 'gill-books'. A telson is present as a long caudal spine. Development is via a 'trilobite' larva, bearing a resemblance to the extinct trilobites. The example below, the horseshoe, or king, crab, is the only living member of the group.

Limulus.

CLASS ARACHNIDA

Arthropods in which the body, in living species, consists of a prosoma, or cephalothorax, of six segments, and an opisthosoma (abdomen) of thirteen segments, which may be divided into two regions, mesosoma and metasoma. In some groups, segmentation is not apparent externally. The prosoma bears one pair of chelicerae, one pair of pedipalps, and typically four pairs of legs, of which the first pair may have a tactile function. True jaws are absent. Eyes are often present, but these are not of a compound nature. Gonopores are present on the second segment of the opisthosoma. The opisthosoma is without appendages except for the pectines of scorpions and the spinnerets of spiders. Respiratory exchange is through 'gill-' or 'lung-books'. Some species have a few tracheae. Development is usually direct.

Order Scorpiones (scorpions): e.g. *Scorpio, Tityus.*
Order Pseudoscorpiones (false scorpions): e.g. *Chelifer, Chthonius.*
Order Uropygi (whip scorpions): e.g. *Mastigoproctus.*
Order Schizomida: e.g. *Schizomus.*
Order Amblypygi (tailless whip scorpions): e.g. *Damon.*
Order Palpigradi (micro whip scorpions): e.g. *Koenenia.*
Order Ricinulei: e.g. *Ricinoides.*
Order Solifugae (wind scorpions): e.g. *Galeodes.*
Order Opiliones (harvest spiders): e.g. *Phalangium.*
Order Araneae (spiders): e.g. *Araneus, Atypus, Latrodectus, Lycosa.*
Order Acari (mites and ticks): e.g. *Ixodes, Acarus, Sarcoptes.*

CLASS PYCNOGONIDA (Pantopoda)
Marine arthropods, typically with thin bodies. The head typically bears one pair of chelicerae, one pair of pedipalps, one pair of ovigerous legs, used by the male for carrying eggs, and one pair of walking legs. A sucking proboscis is typically present. Four eyes are present. The thorax has three segments, each of which bears a pair of legs. The abdomen is rudimentary. There are no respiratory structures. Larvae have two or three pairs of legs.
    e.g. *Nymphon, Pycnogonum.*

CLASS PENTASTOMIDA
The pentastomids form a group considered by some to be degenerate mites, by others to be basically primitive types and designated as a separate phylum. The animals are blood-sucking parasites, especially of the respiratory passages of vertebrates. The adult body is elongate, with annulations, and bearing two pairs of claws close to the mouth. Circulatory and excretory systems are absent.

Respiratory exchange is via scattered air pores. Larvae are mite-like, with four to six pairs of clawed legs.

e.g. *Linguatula*.

CLASS TARDIGRADA

Another group sometimes considered as a separate phylum. The minute body consists of one head segment and five trunk segments, four of which each bear a pair of clawed parapodia-like legs. The mouth has a pair of chitinous stylets. The non-chitinous cuticle bears projecting spines. Circulatory and respiratory structures are absent. Development is usually direct.

e.g. *Macrobiotus*.

The five remaining phyla of the animal kingdom form the deuterostomial coelomates. In these, the anus develops at the position of the embryonic blastopore, and cleavage is typically indeterminate. Development of the coelom is by enterocoely. Segmentation is shown only in the phylum Chordata.

PHYLUM ECHINODERMATA

Marine animals showing radial symmetry in the adult. The symmetry is basically pentamerous with five radii. In some forms, bilateral symmetry is superimposed on the radial. Larval forms are bilateral, and bear ciliated bands. In the adult, numerous small tube-feet (podia), typically for locomotion, are present on either side of ambulacral grooves on the oral side. The dermis has, embedded in it, calcareous plates. The nervous system is simple, without elaborate sensory structures. Specialized excretory organs are not present. As well as a type of blood system, an extensive water vascular system is present, typically with an external opening (madreporite).

SUBPHYLUM PELMATAZOA

Echinoderms which are stalked and sessile for part or all of life. The oral surface is uppermost, and bears the anus as well as the mouth. Ambulacral grooves and podia are used for feeding.

CLASS CRINOIDEA – the sea lilies

The only living group of pelmatazoans. The podia are without suckers. There is no madreporite. Skeletal material is principally on the aboral side, and forms large ossicles.

e.g. *Metacrinus, Antedon.*

SUBPHYLUM ELEUTHEROZOA

Echinoderms which are not stalked. The oral surface is lowermost, or to one side. Ambulacral grooves are not used for feeding, and are often enclosed by skeletal material. Podia are used for locomotion. The anus, if present, is aboral.

CLASS ASTEROIDEA – the starfish

Star-shaped echinoderms with open ambulacral grooves. The podia usually have suckers. The madreporite is aboral. Modified pincer-like groups of spines (pedicellariae) are present. Skeletal material is either in the form of a network, or as a more or less continuous shell.

e.g. *Astropecten, Solaster, Asterias.*

CLASS OPHIUROIDEA – the brittle stars

Star-shaped echinoderms with the central disc clearly distinct from the radiating arms, which are narrow. The podia are without suckers. Anus and pedicellariae are absent. The madreporite is on the oral side. Skeletal material typically forms articulating plates.

e.g. *Ophiura, Ophiothrix, Gorgonocephalus.*

CLASS ECHINOIDEA – the sea urchins

More or less spherical echinoderms, some flattened, with the calcareous plates forming a complete shell, or test. The whole surface, except for a small dorsal area containing the anus and madreporite, is equivalent to the oral surface of starfish. The podia have suckers. Long spines and pedicellariae are present.

e.g. *Diadema, Echinus, Clypeaster, Echinocardium.*

CLASS HOLOTHUROIDEA – the sea cucumbers

Elongate, cylindrical echinoderms, showing bilateral symmetry, superimposed upon the radial symmetry, and without arms. The anterior end has basically ten tentacles surrounding the mouth. Five ambulacra are present, each of which may have two rows of podia. Three of the ambulacra are more or less ventral, the other two are dorsal. Spines and pedicellariae are absent. The body wall is leathery with a few spicules.

e.g. *Holothuria, Cucumaria, Labidoplax.*

PHYLUM CHAETOGNATHA – the arrow-worms

Generally small, transparent, planktonic animals. The body is elongate, and is divided into head, trunk, and a true, post-anal tail. The head has a pair of eyes and two groups of chitinous jaws. Lateral and caudal fins are present on the trunk and tail. There are no specialized organs of respiration or excretion. There is no vascular system. The body wall contains muscle cells of a characteristic type, having a slight resemblance to those of nematodes. The animals are hermaphrodite but cross-fertilization usually occurs. Development is via free-swimming larvae.

e.g. *Sagitta.*

PHYLUM POGONOPHORA – the beard-worms

Solitary, tube-dwelling, marine animals. The long body is extremely thin, and consists of three basic regions. The anterior protosome bears up to 200 coelomate tentacles. These are lined with numerous finger-like pinnules. Behind the protosome is a short mesosome, which is followed by a long metasome. The first portion of the metasome has dorsal cilia and ventral adhesive papillae. An alimentary system is totally absent in the adult, even a mouth being absent. Feeding is probably by the use of the pinnulate tentacles, with extracellular digestion. A vascular system, with a muscular heart, is present. The nervous system is solid and consists of a 'brain' in the protosome, a number of nerves to the tentacles, and a dorsal nerve tract. The sexes are separate. Some species develop via larvae which possess a gut for a short period.

e.g. *Siboglinum, Spirobrachia.*

PHYLUM HEMICHORDATA

Coelomate animals, typically either worm-like or polyp-like. The body consists of three regions: protosome, mesosome, and metasome, each containing a pair of coeloms. The mouth occurs between the protosome and mesosome. The metasome typically has gill slits. The nervous system is mainly solid, but the portion in the mesosome shows some evidence of a hollow nature. The anterior part of the alimentary canal has a dorsal hollow projection strengthening the protosome. This structure is considered by some authorities to be a

75

primitive notochord, and thus the hemichordates would then possess the three basic characteristics that would warrant inclusion of the group in the phylum Chordata. The blood system is typically open, with a contractile heart. Development is via a tornarian larva which shows distinct affinities with the larvae of echinoderms.

CLASS ENTEROPNEUSTA – the acorn-worms
Worm-like hemichordates, with a straight alimentary canal, and numerous gill slits. The epidermis is soft and ciliated. The animals are solitary, burrowing forms.
   e.g. *Balanoglossus, Saccoglossus.*

CLASS PTEROBRANCHIA
Polyp-like hemichordates, with a recurved alimentary canal. Gill slits are few or absent. The mesosome bears two or more ciliated, tentaculate arms. The animals are colonial, and (except *Atubaria*) live in a common secreted case, the coenecium. There are only three known genera.
   Rhabdopleura, Cephalodiscus, Atubaria.

CLASS PLANCTOSPHAEROIDEA
This class was created to accommodate a few larval forms of unknown adults. The larvae appear to be highly modified tornaria, with complex ciliated tracts.
   e.g. *Planctosphaera.*

PHYLUM CHORDATA
The members of the phylum Chordata are characterized by three distinctive features which are present at some stage of development:
1. The wall of the pharynx is perforated by gill slits. In the more primitive groups of chordates, the gill slits are bounded by ciliated cells, and function primarily

for the filtration of food particles from water. In more advanced aquatic groups the gill slits function as respiratory structures, while in the terrestrial chordates they disappear in the adult stages, or are modified for functions other than respiratory.

2. A notochord is present. This is an unsegmented, fibrous rod along the length of the body, dorsal to the intestine. The notochord gives support to the body, and in advanced groups is wholly or partially replaced by a vertebral column of cartilage or bone in the adult.

3. The central nervous system consists of a dorsal, hollow nerve cord above the notochord. In non-chordates, the central nervous system, if present, is typically ventral and solid. In forms in which the notochord is replaced by a vertebral column, the nerve cord becomes enclosed within the vertebral column.

SUBPHYLUM UROCHORDATA (Tunicata) – the sea squirts
Sessile or pelagic, sac-like animals with no evidence of segmentation of the body in the adult. The body is enclosed within a 'test', or 'tunic', which has two openings, an anterior mouth and a dorsal atriopore. A ciliated tract, the endostyle, is present along the ventral side of the pharynx which is perforated by numerous gill slits. The free-swimming 'tadpole' larvae possess the full chordate characters of pharyngeal gill slits, notochord, and dorsal, hollow nerve cord. In addition, a tail is present which has a segmental arrangement of muscles. All the urochordates are marine.

CLASS ASCIDIACEA
The adults are sessile, and solitary or colonial. Most species live in shallow waters.

e.g. *Morcellium, Ciona, Botrylus*.

CLASS THALIACEA

Pelagic forms, solitary or colonial. Circular muscle bands are present which are used in locomotion.

e.g. *Pyrosoma, Doliolum, Salpa.*

CLASS LARVACEA

Minute, pelagic forms, in which the adult retains the larval tail with notochord and dorsal, hollow nerve cord.

e.g. *Oikopleura.*

SUBPHYLUM CEPHALOCHORDATA (Acrania)

This subphylum contains the most primitive animals which possess the full chordate characters in the adult. The notochord remains as such throughout life. The body is segmented and fish-like in shape, but without cranium or paired fins. There are only three genera.

e.g. *Amphioxus.*

SUBPHYLUM VERTEBRATA (Craniata)

Segmented chordates, in which the notochord is replaced by a vertebral column of cartilage or bone. The anterior end of the nerve cord is developed into a highly organized brain which is housed in a skeletal box, the cranium. The structure of the cranium, or skull, is used extensively in the detailed classification of the vertebrates.

SUPERCLASS AGNATHA

Vertebrates which do not possess jaws. A number of fossil agnathans are known which had heavily armoured bodies, but living forms have no external skeleton. All the living species belong to a single order, and are commonly known as lampreys and hagfish. The larval stage, the ammocoete larva, shows distinct similarities to the cephalochordates.

e.g. *Petromyzon, Lampetra, Myxine.*

SUPERCLASS GNATHOSTOMATA

Vertebrates with articulating jaws of skeletal material, typically bearing teeth. The first two classes of gnathostomes are sometimes grouped together as Pisces, the fish. These two classes have a number of characteristics in common. Typically, they possess two pairs of lateral fins, and a finned tail for propulsion in water. Associated with an extremely active life, the pharyngeal gill slits and the jaws have become enlarged, due to the increased need for oxygen and nutrients.

CLASS CHONDRICHTHYES (Elasmobranchii)

The skeleton is cartilaginous, no bone being present. Typically there is no operculum covering the external openings of the gill slits. The tail is usually heterocercal, i.e. the portion of fin below the vertebral column is larger than that above the vertebral column. The body surface is covered with placoid scales (dermal denticles).

SUBCLASS SELACHII – Typical elasmobranchs as defined by the characteristics given above. Skates, rays, and sharks.

e.g. *Heterodontus, Scyliorhinus, Raja, Torpedo, Cetorhinus.*

SUBCLASS BRADYODONTI – Somewhat atypical types in that, among a number of differences, there is an operculum covering the external gill slits, and the mouth is reduced to a small aperture.

e.g. *Chimaera.*

CLASS OSTEICHTHYES

The skeleton is bony. An operculum is present. The

tail is typically homocercal, i.e. with equal portions of fin above and below the vertebral column. The body surface is covered with overlapping scales, primitively bony and covered by a thin layer of skin. In most modern forms the bony element of the scales is lacking. Internally, a swim bladder, derived from the gut and containing air, is present.

SUBCLASS ACTINOPTERYGII – The skeletal support of the fins consists of a number of radiating rays.

e.g. *Polypterus, Acipenser, Amia, Lepidosteus, Clupea, Anguilla, Gadus, Solea.*

SUBCLASS CROSSOPTERYGII (Choanichthyes) – The paired fins have a central skeletal support consisting of a number of bones. Coelacanth and lung-fish.

e.g. *Latimeria, Protopterus*

The four remaining classes in the superclass Gnathostomata are collectively known as the Tetrapoda, the 'four-footed' animals. The four limbs have bony skeletons based on a pentadactyl limb plan. The development of such a limb aided the invasion of land by the vertebrates.

CLASS AMPHIBIA

Tetrapods which have a naked skin in that there are no epidermal outgrowths such as scales, feathers, or hairs. The amphibians are not entirely independent of the aquatic environment, and the majority of them must return to water to breed. Fertilization is external, eggs and sperm being shed simultaneously into the water. Development is via a typically free-swimming larva (tadpole). There are usually no gills in the adult stage.

SUBCLASS URODELA (Caudata) – Newts and salamanders. Amphibians possessing normal legs and a tail.

e.g. *Proteus, Cryptobranchus, Salamandra, Triturus, Amblystoma.*

SUBCLASS ANURA (Salientia) – Frogs and toads. Amphibians specialized for jumping and climbing, although some are entirely aquatic. The hind legs are elongated, and there is no tail in the adult.

e.g. *Pipa, Xenopus, Rana, Bufo, Hyla.*

SUBCLASS APODA (Caecilia) – Amphibians specialized for burrowing. They are elongated, without legs or eyes.

e.g. *Ichthyophis.*

CLASS REPTILIA

Tetrapods in which the body is covered by a horny skin. Fertilization is internal. Eggs, enclosed in a leathery shell, are laid on land. There is no free-living larval stage. A few species are viviparous. The living species are contained within four orders.

SUBCLASS ANAPSIDA – There are no holes in the temporal region of the skull.

Order Chelonia (tortoises and turtles): e.g. *Testudo, Chelone.*

SUBCLASS DIAPSIDA – There are two holes in the temporal region of the skull. The inclusion of the Squamata in this subclass is questionable. In this group there has been considerable modification of skull structure. Only one temporal fossa is present in the Squamata, but this condition may have arisen by the loss of bones between fossae.

Order Rhynchocephalia (the tuatara): *Sphenodon*.

Order Squamata (lizards and snakes): e.g. *Lacerta, Gecko, Chamaeleo, Iguana, Python, Vipera, Natrix*.

Order Crocodilia (crocodiles): e.g. *Crocodilus, Alligator, Caiman, Gavialis*.

CLASS AVES – the birds

The birds are characterized, principally, by the presence of feathers and a beak, both of which evolved from reptilian scales. In most, the fore-limbs are modified for flight and only the hind-limbs are used for terrestrial locomotion. In a few groups the power of flight has been lost. Birds are oviparous, and the eggs are enclosed in a hard, but permeable, shell. Living species have no teeth. All living species are included in a single subclass.

Subclass Neornithes – the modern birds.

Superorder Palaeognathae (flightless birds):
e.g. *Struthio, Apteryx, Rhea*.

Superorder Neognathae (flying birds):
e.g. *Spheniscus, Columba, Anas, Falco, Turdus*.

CLASS MAMMALIA

The main distinguishing characteristics of the mammals are the presence of hair and the presence of mammary glands. Typically hair forms a more or less complete covering of the body. Although, of the living tetrapods, only the mammals possess hair, it is possible that some of the mammal-like reptiles of the Jurassic had also developed hair. Mammary glands are present under the skin on the ventral side of the body. They become functional only in the female.

SUBCLASS PROTOTHERIA – The prototherians are the only egg-laying mammals. The egg is enclosed in a leathery shell. The ducts of the mammary glands do not unite to form nipples, as in other mammals, but open individually over a large area of the ventral surface. External ears are not present. Posteriorly, there is a single opening, the cloaca.

Order Monotremata: e.g. *Tachyglossus, Ornithorhynchus.*

SUBCLASS THERIA – the viviparous mammals. The remainder of the mammals are included in this subclass. The mammary glands open to the exterior via fully developed nipples. There are typically two posterior openings, the anus and the urinogenital aperture.

INFRACLASS METATHERIA – The young are born in a very immature condition, and develop further in an abdominal pouch, the marsupium, more or less securely attached to the nipples within the pouch.

Order Marsupialia (the marsupials): e.g. *Macropus, Didelphis, Perameles.*

INFRACLASS EUTHERIA (Placentalia) – The young develop to a relatively mature condition within the uterus, attached to the mother by an allantoic placenta. All the remaining mammals belong to this infraclass.

Order Insectivora (shrews, moles, hedgehogs, tenrecs): e.g. *Sorex, Erinaceus, Talpa.*

Order Chiroptera (bats): e.g. *Pteropus, Myotis, Rhinolophus.*

Order Dermoptera (flying lemurs): e.g. *Cynocephalus.*

Order Primates (lemurs, lorises, monkeys, apes, man):
e.g. *Tupaia, Macaca, Cebus, Pan, Homo.*

Order Edentata (armadillos, anteaters, sloths): e.g. *Dasypus, Myrmecophaga, Bradypus.*

Order Pholidota (pangolins): e.g. *Manis*.

Order Lagomorpha (rabbits, hares): e.g. *Lepus, Oryctolagus*.

Order Rodentia (rodents): e.g. *Sciurus, Rattus, Mus, Cavia, Myocastor*.

Order Cetacea (whales, dolphins): e.g. *Physeter, Delphinus, Balaenoptera*.

Order Carnivora (carnivores): e.g. *Canis, Ursus, Mustela, Lutra, Felis*.

Order Pinnipedia (seals): e.g. *Zalophus, Phoca, Odobenus*.

Order Tubulidentata (aardvark): *Orycteropus*.

Order Proboscidea (elephants): e.g. *Loxodonta*.

Order Hyracoidea (hyraxes): e.g. *Procavia*.

Order Sirenia (sea cows): e.g. *Dugong*.

Order Perissodactyla (odd-toed ungulates): e.g. *Equus, Tapirus, Rhinoceros*.

Order Artiodactyla (even-toed ungulates): e.g. *Sus, Camelus, Dama, Giraffa, Bos, Gazella, Ovis*.

CLASSIFICATION LIST OF THE ANIMAL KINGDOM AS DESCRIBED IN THE FOREGOING SECTION

Kingdom Animalia
  Subkingdom Protozoa
    Phylum Protozoa
        Class Mastigophora
          Subclass Phytomastigina
          Subclass Zoomastigina
        Class Rhizopoda
        Class Sporozoa
          Subclass Telosporidia
          Subclass Neosporidia
        Class Ciliophora
          Subclass Ciliata
          Subclass Suctoria
  Subkingdom Mesozoa
    Phylum Mesozoa
  Subkingdom Parazoa
    Phylum Porifera
        Class Calcarea
        Class Hexactinellida
        Class Demospongiae
  Subkingdom Metazoa
    Phylum Cnidaria
        Class Hydrozoa
        Class Scyphozoa
        Class Anthozoa
          Subclass Alcyonaria

Subclass Zoantharia
Phylum Ctenophora
   Class Tentaculata
   Class Nuda
Phylum Platyhelminthes
   Class Turbellaria
   Class Trematoda
      Subclass Monogenea
      Subclass Digenea
      Subclass Aspidogastrea
   Class Cestoda
      Subclass Cestodaria
      Subclass Eucestoda
Phylum Nemertea
   Class Anopla
   Class Enopla
Phylum Acanthocephala
Phylum Aschelminthes
   Class Rotifera
   Class Gastrotricha
   Class Kinorhyncha
   Class Priapulida
   Class Nematoda
   Class Nematomorpha
Phylum Entoprocta
Phylum Phoronida
Phylum Ectoprocta
   Class Phylactolaemata
   Class Gymnolaemata
Phylum Brachiopoda
   Class Inarticulata
   Class Articulata
Phylum Sipunculida
Phylum Echiuroidea

Phylum Mollusca
    Class Amphineura
        Subclass Monoplacophora
        Subclass Polyplacophora
        Subclass Aplacophora
    Class Gastropoda
        Subclass Prosobranchia
        Subclass Opisthobranchia
        Subclass Pulmonata
    Class Scaphopoda
    Class Bivalvia
        Subclass Protobranchia
        Subclass Lamellibranchia
        Subclass Septibranchia
    Class Cephalopoda
        Subclass Tetrabranchiata
        Subclass Dibranchiata
Phylum Annelida
    Class Polychaeta
    Class Mysostomaria
    Class Archiannelida
    Class Oligochaeta
    Class Hirudinea
Phylum Arthropoda
    Class Onychophora
    Class Pauropoda
    Class Diplopoda
        Subclass Pselaphognatha
        Subclass Chilognatha
    Class Chilopoda
        Subclass Epimorpha
        Subclass Anamorpha
    Class Symphyla
    Class Insecta

Subclass Apterygota
  Order Protura
  Order Diplura
  Order Thysanura
  Order Collembola
Subclass Pterygota
  Division Exopterygota
    Order Ephemeroptera
    Order Odonata
    Order Dictyoptera
    Order Isoptera
    Order Zoraptera
    Order Plecoptera
    Order Grylloblattodea
    Order Phasmida
    Order Orthoptera
    Order Embioptera
    Order Dermaptera
    Order Psocoptera
    Order Mallophaga
    Order Siphunculata
    Order Thysanoptera
    Order Hemiptera
  Division Endopterygota
    Order Neuroptera
    Order Coleoptera
    Order Strepsiptera
    Order Mecoptera
    Order Trichoptera
    Order Zeugloptera
    Order Lepidoptera
    Order Diptera
    Order Siphonaptera
    Order Hymenoptera

Class Crustacea
    Subclass Branchiopoda
    Subclass Cephalocarida
    Subclass Ostracoda
    Subclass Copepoda
    Subclass Mystacocarida
    Subclass Branchiura
    Subclass Cirripedia
    Subclass Malacostraca
        Superorder Leptostraca
        Superorder Syncarida
        Superorder Hoplocarida
        Superorder Peracarida
        Superorder Pancarida
        Superorder Eucarida
Class Merostomata
Class Arachnida
        Order Scorpiones
        Order Pseudoscorpiones
        Order Uropygi
        Order Schizomida
        Order Amblypygi
        Order Palpigradi
        Order Ricinulei
        Order Solifugae
        Order Opiliones
        Order Araneae
        Order Acari
Class Pycnogonida
Class Pentastomida
Class Tardigrada
Phylum Echinodermata
    Subphylum Pelmatazoa
      Class Crinoidea

Subphylum Eleutherozoa
   Class Asteroidea
   Class Ophiuroidea
   Class Echinoidea
   Class Holothuroidea
Phylum Chaetognatha
Phylum Pogonophora
Phylum Hemichordata
   Class Enteropneusta
   Class Pterobranchia
   Class Planctosphaeroidea
Phylum Chordata
  Subphylum Urochordata
   Class Ascidiacea
   Class Thaliacea
   Class Larvacea
  Subphylum Cephalochordata
  Subphylum Vertebrata
   Superclass Agnatha
   Superclass Gnathostomata
   Class Chondrichthyes
    Subclass Selachii
    Subclass Bradyodonti
   Class Osteichthyes
    Subclass Actinopterygii
    Subclass Crossopterygii
   Class Amphibia
    Subclass Urodela
    Subclass Anura
    Subclass Apoda
   Class Reptilia
    Subclass Anapsida
      Order Chelonia
    Subclass Diapsida

      Order Rhynchocephalia
      Order Squamata
      Order Crocodilia
Class Aves
  Subclass Neornithes
    Superorder Palaeognathae
    Superorder Neognathae
Class Mammalia
  Subclass Prototheria
      Order Monotremata
  Subclass Theria
    Infraclass Metatheria
      Order Marsupialia
    Infraclass Eutheria
      Order Insectivora
      Order Chiroptera
      Order Dermoptera
      Order Primates
      Order Edentata
      Order Pholidota
      Order Lagomorpha
      Order Rodentia
      Order Cetacea
      Order Carnivora
      Order Pinnipedia
      Order Tubulidentata
      Order Proboscidea
      Order Hyracoidea
      Order Sirenia
      Order Perissodactyla
      Order Artiodactyla

APPENDIX

Identification Keys

A key is an artificial device of use in the identification of specimens. A key works by the elimination of more and more types until the required identification is achieved. The usual form of a key is a dichotomous layout in which, at each stage, there is a choice between (usually) two alternative characteristics, only one of which will apply to the specimen in question. It must be remembered that a key is an *artificial* device, and does not necessarily indicate any true relationships between types. For instance, a key for the identification of adult insects would probably, at an early stage, include a choice between 'winged' and 'wingless'. This would not, however, be dividing the insects into the subclasses Apterygota and Pterygota, since a number of wingless insects are included in the subclass Pterygota, having developed the wingless condition secondarily. Often, the characteristics used in a key are of a trivial nature, e.g. colour, relative size and proportions, and so on.

The basic form of a dichotomous key is illustrated in the example below, which is a simple key to the adults of the classes of the superclass Gnathostomata:

1 ⎰ Skeleton entirely cartilaginous ...... Chondrichthyes
  ⎱ Skeleton of bony material .... go to 2

2 ⎰ With gill slits covered by operculum Osteichthyes
  ⎱ Without gill slits .... go to 3

3 ⎰ Skin without scales, feathers, or hair Amphibia
  ⎱ Skin with scales, feathers, or hair ... go to 4

4 ⎰ Skin with scales, but not feathers or
      hair........................... Reptilia
  ⎱ Feathers or hair present .... go to 5

5 ⎰ Feathers present .... Aves
  ⎱ Hair present .... Mammalia

In this example, at '1' there is a choice between cartilaginous and bony skeletons. If the specimen in question has a cartilaginous skeleton, then it belongs to the class Chondrichthyes. If the skeleton is bony, one proceeds to '2', where there is a choice between the presence or absence of gill slits, presence indicating that the specimen is of the class Osteichthyes, absence necessitating moving on to '3', and so on.

In the above example, the choices are sequential – in order to reach the final choice, one passes through all the preceding choices. This is not usually the case; in more comprehensive keys, an early choice eliminates a large number of the succeeding choices. This is illustrated in the following example, which is a key to the classes and subclasses of the phylum Mollusca. Two possible arrangements of the same key are given.

1 { Molluscs with two or more tentacles 2
    Molluscs without tentacles 7

2 { Eyes present 3
    Eyes absent . . . . Class Scaphopoda

3 { One or two pairs of tentacles . . . . Class Gastropoda – 4
    Eight or more tentacles . . . . Class Cephalopoda – 6

4 { With full, 180° torsion 5
    With 90° or 180° detorsion . . . . Subclass Opisthobranchia

5 { With one pair of tentacles . . . . Subclass Prosobranchia
    With two pairs of tentacles . . . . Subclass Pulmonata

6 { With numerous tentacles, and
    external shell . . . . Subclass Tetrabranchiata
    With eight or ten tentacles; shell,
    if present, is internal* . . . . Subclass Dibranchiata

7 { Shell consisting of two lateral valves . Class Bivalvia – 8
    Shell, if present, is dorsal, and single
    or of eight plates . . . . Class Amphineura – 9

8 { Ctenidia consist of flat gill filaments Subclass Protobranchia
    Gill filaments reflected forming
    W-shaped ctenidia . . . . Subclass Lamellibranchia
    Ctenidia modified as muscular,
    perforated septa . . . . Subclass Septibranchia

9 { With single shell plate . . . . Subclass Monoplacophora
    With eight shell plates . . . . Subclass Polyplacophora
    Shell plates absent . . . . Subclass Aplacophora

* *Argonauta*, belonging to this subclass, is an exception to this in that the female produces a papery external shell.

I. Molluscs with two or more tentacles
  A. Eyes present
      1. One or two pairs of tentacles   Class Gastropoda
        a. With full, 180° torsion
          i. With one pair of
            tentacles   Subclass Prosobranchia
          ii. With two pairs of
            tentacles   Subclass Pulmonata
        b. With 90° or 180°
          detorsion   Subclass Opisthobranchia
      2. Eight or more tentacles   Class Cephalopoda
        a. With numerous tentacles,
          and external shell   Subclass Tetrabranchiata
        b. With eight or ten
          tentacles; shell, if present,
          is internal*   Subclass Dibranchiata
  B. Eyes absent   Class Scaphopoda
II. Molluscs without tentacles
  A. Shell consisting of two lateral
    valves   Class Bivalvia
      1. Ctenidia consist of flat
        gill filaments   Subclass Protobranchia
      2. Gill filaments reflected
        forming W-shaped ctenidia   Subclass Lamellibranchia
      3. Ctenidia modified as
        muscular, perforated septa   Subclass Septibranchia
  B. Shell, if present, is dorsal,
    and single or of eight plates   Class Amphineura
      1. With single shell plate   Subclass **Monoplacophora**
      2. With eight shell plates   Subclass **Polyplacophora**
      3. Shell plates absent   Subclass **Aplacophora**

* See footnote on p. 94.

SELECTED BIBLIOGRAPHY

This short bibliography is divided into three sections. Firstly, works on the principles and functions of classification; secondly, readings relevant to the section on recent techniques; and thirdly, systematic works on the variety of animal life. Many of the 'A' level standard text books also give surveys of the animal kingdom, at least at the higher levels of classification. Only a few of the larger, more comprehensive works are listed here, together with Rothschild's classification list of the animal kingdom.

Principles and Functions

CALMAN, W. T. *The Classification of Animals*. Methuen, London, 1949.

HEYWOOD, V. H. *Plant Taxonomy*. Arnold, London. 1967.

HUXLEY, J. S. (Editor). *The New Systematics*. Oxford University Press. 1940.

MAYR, E., LINSLEY, E. G. and USINGER, R. L. *Methods and Principles of Systematic Zoology*. McGraw-Hill, New York. 1953.

SIMPSON, G. G. The Principles of Classification and a Classification of Mammals. *Bulletin of the American Museum of Natural History,* vol. *85.* 1945.

SIMPSON, G. G. *Principles of Animal Taxonomy*. Columbia University Press: Oxford University Press. 1961.

Recent Techniques

COLE, A. J. (Editor). *Numerical Taxonomy*. Academic Press, London and New York. 1968.

ENGLE, R. L., Jr. and WOODS, K. R. Comparative Biochemistry and Embryology. In *The Plasma Proteins,* Volume 2, edited by F. W. Putnam. Academic Press, New York and London. 1960.

HAWKES, J. G. (Editor). *Chemotaxonomy and Serotaxonomy.* Academic Press, London and New York. 1968.

HOYER, B. H., MCCARTHY, B. J. and BOLTON, E. T. A Molecular Approach in the Systematics of Higher Organisms. *Science,* vol. *144,* 959–967. 1964.

SOKAL, R. R. Numerical Taxonomy. *Scientific American,* vol. *215,* 106–116. 1966.

Variety of Animal Life

BORRADAILE, L. A., EASTHAM, L. E. S., POTTS, F. A. and SAUNDERS, J. T. *The Invertebrata.* (Fourth Edition.) Cambridge University Press. 1961.

HYMAN, L. H. *The Invertebrates.* Volumes I–IV so far published. McGraw-Hill, New York and London. 1940—.

Larousse Encyclopedia of Animal Life. Paul Hamlyn, London. 1967.

ROTHSCHILD, LORD. *A Classification of Living Animals.* (Second Edition.) Longmans, London. 1965.

YOUNG, J. Z. *The Life of Vertebrates.* (Second Edition.) Oxford University Press. 1962.

INDEX

99